Tales of Total Forgiveness

To

Pastor Richard and Rajinder,

Thank you both for all your
support.

Love from,

E. Parmar.

19. Dec. 2004

Also by R. T. Kendall

The Anointing – Yesterday, Today, Tomorrow
The Day the World Changed
The Gift of Giving
In Pursuit of His Glory
Pure Joy
The Sensitivity of the Spirit
Thanking God
The Thorn in the Flesh
Total Forgiveness
Worshipping God

Compiled and edited by Louise and R. T. Kendall

Great Christian Prayers:
From Two Thousand Years of Christian Faith

Also by Julia Fisher

Our Little Secret (with Tori Dante)

Tales of
Total Forgiveness

R. T. Kendall and Julia Fisher

Hodder & Stoughton
LONDON SYDNEY AUCKLAND

Unless otherwise indicated, Scripture quotations are taken from the
HOLY BIBLE, NEW INTERNATIONAL VERSION. Copyright © 1973, 1978,
1984 by International Bible Society. Used by permission of Hodder
& Stoughton. All rights reserved. 'NIV' is a registered trademark of
International Bible Society. UK trademark number 1448790.

First published in Great Britain in 2004

Lyrics to 'True Love' by David Ruis © Mercy/Vineyard Publishing.
Administered by CopyCare, P.O. Box 77, Hailsham, BN27 3EF.
Used by permission.

10 9 8 7 6 5 4 3 2 1

British Library Cataloguing in Publication Data
A record for this book is available from the British Library

ISBN 0 340 86327 7

Typeset in Bembo by Avon DataSet Ltd,
Bidford-on-Avon, Warwickshire

Printed and bound in Great Britain by
Bookmarque Ltd, Croydon, Surrey

The paper and board used in this paperback are natural recyclable
products made from wood grown in sustainable forests.
The manufacturing processes conform to the environmental
regulations of the country of origin.

Hodder & Stoughton
A Division of Hodder Headline Ltd
338 Euston Road
London NW1 3BH
www.madaboutbooks.com

Dedicated to Canon Andrew White

Contents

Preface

'Could you write the preface, Julia, I am sure I will approve and we will jointly sign it.'

Well, with an invitation like that how else can I start but by thanking RT for inviting me to share in the writing of this book! RT is one of the most honest people I know. To meet a respected theologian who is willing to share his own spiritual struggles in the public arena is rare indeed. But that's what RT did in his book, *Total Forgiveness*. I remember reading the manuscript and being amazed at the candid way in which it had been written. This was no sermon. This was raw experience. But RT is a man who has a heart to help others by sharing from his own experience – in other words, his theology works! So thank you RT!

But wait a minute, this book has written itself! Each story shared represents a person responding to the simple question, 'Would you be willing to share your story of forgiveness in a book?' As RT says, to share such a story is sometimes impossible. Where it is possible it has to be done with respect to all involved. But everybody who has told their stories here has done so gladly . . . for each one, forgiving those who have hurt them has opened the door and released them from a world of fear and mistrust, to a world of freedom and life! So thank you to each and every one – an entire book could have been devoted to you all!

But it's one thing writing a book – it's quite another thing finding a suitable publisher. In David Moloney we have not only a publisher with an eye for a good story, but also a true friend. David is a publisher with integrity. Thank you, David, for gently steering this project along, and for your encouragement and advice which is always delivered in the most tactful manner possible! We appreciate you.

We have dedicated this book to Andrew White. Andrew is currently a Canon at Coventry Cathedral and one of the directors of their International Centre for Reconciliation. Andrew understands the importance of forgiveness and reconciliation. His work in the Middle East, in Israel and the West Bank in particular, not to mention Iraq, has been an inspiration. Andrew, our paths have interwoven thus far; may they continue to do so.

RT Kendall and Julia Fisher
August 2004

Introduction

I was not prepared for the extraordinary stories which Julia Fisher has not only compiled but beautifully written up and presented in this book. You are about to embark upon an adventure in witnessing the grace of God beyond anything you have possibly ever come across. It is one thing to know of God's forgiveness of all our sins, a truth that we must never take for granted; and yet it is quite another to learn of true, unembellished accounts of people who have forgiven others when they have been so deeply and unjustly wronged.

After Hodder & Stoughton published my book *Total Forgiveness* a few years ago we began to hear of stories of people who had unusual experiences regarding having to forgive deep hurts, great injustices and all sorts of unfair treatment. The more we heard the more we felt that such testimonies ought to be made available to the public. I also knew that Julia Fisher was in contact with various people who had stories to tell. She was my only choice as one who could make the present book a possibility. And so here it is!

The truth is, we all have a story to tell. Not all of us will have the privilege of seeing our own struggles put into print. Furthermore, not all stories *can* be told, partly because one does not want to reveal the identity of people who could be embarrassed or compromised, and partly because one of the principles of *total* forgiveness is that you refuse to tell who hurt you and what they did to you. But there are times when the truth can be revealed, partly if the accounts are in the public domain to some extent anyway and partly because all the parties involved are thrilled for the story to be known. The stories that Julia has written about therefore are not cases of people telling what happened in order to punish the wrong-doer or get vengeance; far from it. These are stories of triumph – indeed, the triumph of God's grace in their lives. They tell what happened and what they had to forgive in order to encourage others to know the blissful liberation that comes when one truly does totally forgive.

This book is not a compilation of testimonies of those who have read my own book *Total Forgiveness*. What follows are accounts from people who have forgiven – who never even heard of my book. These stories go to show that there have been people across the years and the centuries who have taken the teachings of Jesus seriously and have discovered the joy of practising what Jesus taught and preached.

The reason for this book therefore is to spread the good news of total forgiveness, to let the world know the import-ance of forgiving others and the joy that follows when you do. We hope that if *you* have struggled with this issue that this book will give you the push you need to cross over into the supernatural – to do what indeed defies a natural explanation of things – and do what Jesus told us to do.

I put it that way for this reason. People have sometimes

said to me, 'I have never seen a miracle. I have heard of great healings and miracles, but I haven't seen any. I am not sure they even exist.' If you therefore have not seen the blind healed or the ears of the deaf unstopped, you can be the first witness of the equivalent of such a miracle: you yourself totally forgive one who has been very, very wrong and unfair. Not because they deserve it but because you deserve to have the privilege. And I can tell you, if you truly forgive that person – totally – for the evil and wicked things they did, you will have achieved the equivalent of a miracle of seeing the dead raised. Because total forgiveness is not something one does naturally; it is the result of the power of the Spirit.

There may be an exception to this. For even non-Christians are discovering the benefit of forgiving others. Whether such people do it *totally* I do not know, but it is true that some of those who are not Christians have discovered that the person who derives the greatest benefit from forgiving others is not the one who gets forgiven but the one who does the forgiving. This has been achieved therefore, from what I can tell, by those without the aid of the Holy Spirit's power. But this is not the norm. In the main, I can assure you, those who have been deeply hurt by another and yet managed utterly and totally to forgive them have crossed over into the supernatural and therefore demonstrate the power of God that is as real as when Jesus healed the sick in his day.

This is because the motivation to forgive is provided by Jesus' example and teachings. The power to forgive comes to those who realise God has forgiven them and, in the light of what God has done for us, we cannot but pass this forgiveness on to others. As the Apostle Paul put it, 'Be kind and compassionate to one another, forgiving one another, just as in Christ God forgave you' (Eph. 4:32).

My book *Total Forgiveness* was born in the greatest trial that Louise and I had ever known at the time. People keep asking me to tell what it was I had to forgive. I cannot tell it – ever. After all, the first principle of total forgiveness is that you do not tell who wronged you or what they did. If there were a way of telling what they did without enabling people to figure out who it was and what they did, I would tell it – as Julia freely tells stories in this book. After all, it is thrilling to hear what people have gone through and what they forgave. But in some cases you cannot talk about it – lest it be a subtle way to punish someone. And this is why I cannot ever tell what we went through.

But I can tell you this. It was the best thing that ever happened to me! That I can say without any fear of exaggeration. What was at the time the worst thing that ever happened turned out to be the best thing that ever happened. It is one more proof of my favourite verse in the Bible, 'And we know that all things work together for good to them that love God, to them who are the called according to his purpose' (Rom. 8:28, AV). If I could narrow my twenty-five years at Westminster Chapel down to fifteen minutes – to spotlight my finest hour, it was when my Romanian friend Joseph Tson said lovingly but firmly to me,

> RT, you must totally forgive them. Until you totally forgive them you will be in chains. Release them and you will be released.

I was not prepared for that word. I had decided to tell Joseph what 'they' did partly because I knew he would not tell anybody and partly because I was so sure he would put his arm around me and say, 'RT, you ought to be angry, get it out of your system.' But no. He would not let me off the hook – unless I let others off the hook! 'Faithful are the wounds of a friend' (Prov. 27:6, AV). What 'they' did was the best thing that ever *happened* to me; what Joseph said to me was the greatest thing ever *said* to me; what I was able to do by the power of the Holy Spirit was the wisest and most wonderful thing I ever *did*.

This book has been written to help you to do the same thing – to forgive them totally. Whatever it was. Whoever it was. Wherever it was. Whenever it was. Or for whatever reason they did it.

I wish that I had kept all the letters people have written to me after they read my book *Total Forgiveness*. Except for the obvious possibility of self-aggrandisement it might even have been helpful to print a few in this Introduction from countless unsolicited letters I have received – and continue to receive almost daily – from people who just felt the need to thank me for what my book did for them. This of course is gratifying. But I sometimes feel like a fraud, for all I did was to pass on the basic teaching of Jesus on forgiveness and how Joseph in the Old Testament forgave his brothers for selling him into slavery.

There is one letter, however, I will share as I only read it today – moments before I began to write the Introduction to this book. It was from a couple who with the help of none other than Joseph Tson had adopted a baby from Romania. After the child grew up there were problems that led to an unjust accusation in his school and it became quite serious, even involving a lawsuit. For some reason this couple picked up my book *Total Forgiveness* and when they saw Joseph Tson quoted at the beginning of the book they said it was like Joseph speaking directly to them. They totally forgave. As it happened all ended well but the internal victory that preceded the happy outcome was more important to them.

That is perhaps one of the most important points, as I have been suggesting all along: what it does for the person who forgives – the internal liberty, the feeling of emancipation from bondage and the lightness of spirit that follows totally forgiving.

And yet it isn't easy. When Joseph Tson first said what he did I protested. 'You have no idea,' I started in. Besides, I said, 'I can't.' He replied, 'You can and you must.' I would have to say that practising total forgiveness is *the hardest thing I have ever – ever – had to do.* I do not say it will be easy. Forgiving that authority figure who abused you as a child. Forgiving the one who lied about you and now everybody believes what was said as being the truth. Forgiving the spouse who was unfaithful. Forgiving your best friend who betrayed you. Forgiving that person who promised you the earth and sky and then let you down. Forgiving the person who stole from you. Forgiving the person who is responsible for your being disabled – or ill. Forgiving the rapist. It isn't easy. It is like climbing Mount Everest – few do it. But the reward is incalculable.

This book has been prepared to challenge you to climb Mount Everest. You could say, 'Since few do it, why should I?' I answer: for one thing Jesus told us to. Secondly, why succumb to the herd instinct that makes so many unthinking people follow the masses on their way to confusion and despair? Should you be deprived merely because most people choose such a needless deprivation? By the way, do you ever pray the Lord's Prayer? Do you recall that petition 'Forgive us our trespasses, as we forgive those who have trespassed against us'? I suppose the Lord's Prayer has made liars out of more people than any document in human history. But don't blame Jesus for that! Either mean it or stop praying it. Incidentally, the Greek language that lies behind that petition is rightly to be interpreted 'Forgive us our trespasses *in proportion* to how we forgive others'. Therefore are you happy to be forgiven by God for all of your sins in proportion to how you have forgiven people for what they have done to you? What if God were to say to you, 'I cannot forgive you totally because you have not forgiven them totally'?

It is amazing how the ABCs of Jesus' teaching can be swept under the carpet in our priorities in grasping his message. To read the four Gospels and not see his teaching of forgiveness is like crossing the Atlantic and not seeing the water! Whether it be the Sermon on the Mount or the parables he gave us, so much of what he taught has been overlooked by us. We often read the New Testament in order to see only the teachings that best suit our needs or what coheres with our pet theological points of view.

I have also written a book called *The Sensitivity of the Holy Spirit*. This book is based upon a New Testament teaching that pertains to the 'the *ungrieved* Holy Spirit'. It is based largely on Ephesians 4:30, 'And do not grieve the Holy Spirit of God, with whom you were sealed for the day of redemption'. When the Holy Spirit is not grieved, he is himself – undisturbed. This tells us that the Holy Spirit is sensitive; indeed, he is a very sensitive person. Indeed, he can be easily grieved. The Greek word here means to get one's feelings hurt. The Holy Spirit can get his feelings hurt! This happens when the Holy Spirit – who indwells every Christian (Rom. 8:9) – feels pain when we are bitter, angry, slandering another and hold any kind of a grudge toward someone. The proof is that Paul said so in Ephesians 4:31–2: 'Get rid of all bitterness, rage and anger, brawling and slander, along with every form of malice. Be kind and compassionate to one another, forgiving each other, just as in Christ God forgave you.' And when the Holy Spirit is grieved we lose *presence of mind*, the ability to think clearly and the peace of being in control of your emotions. But when he is *ungrieved* it is like the Dove of the Holy Spirit descending upon us – giving us inner liberty, self-control and clear thinking! It is wonderful. And the best way to ensure that the Holy Spirit in us is ungrieved is, simply, total forgiveness. That's the truth! And it works.

In this brief Introduction I will not of course have the space to go into the details of this issue as found in my book *Total Forgiveness*. But before I introduce Julia Fisher and turn things over to her, please allow me to show how you may know you have totally forgiven that person or people (or whatever) who have injured you or been unjust. There are seven principles.

You don't tell who hurt you or what they did. Why is it that the first thing we want to do when we have been hurt is to find someone who will listen to us and tell them what 'they' did to us? It is our weapon of revenge! We want to punish them. We do it by hurting their credibility or respectability. We don't want them to be loved or liked. We cannot bear the thought that others should admire such people so we 'set the record straight' and make sure our enemy is exposed for what he or she is – we tell what they did.

But we begin the practice of total forgiveness by not telling what they did. This may seem hard. It is hard. But the rule of thumb is *the tongue* and controlling the tongue is the first step towards total forgiveness. God does not tell the world what he knows about us! Thank God for that. For when Jesus died for us on the cross, 'as far as the east is from the west, so far has he removed our transgressions from us' (Ps. 103:12). He will not tell me what he knows about you and thankfully he will not tell you what he knows about me. But when I claim to have forgiven you but tell people what you did, God says 'Whoa! This is not on.' When I have truly forgiven you, I will tell nobody what you did – ever. Unless, of course, there is a situation that invites disclosure, as in this book. But let me repeat, it is not a case of vengeance but of testimony to God's grace. Nobody described in this book is wanting to hurt anybody or make them look bad. We do not tell on them.

There are two exceptions to this principle. First, you may need to tell what happened to you to one other person – for therapeutic reasons. Tell your vicar, pastor, counsellor – someone who will not tell. Secondly, you may need to testify in a court of law lest a person – such as a rapist who is a danger to society – injure another person as well. But the main reason we tell what 'they' did is to get even, to make sure they are punished. This violates the principle from the outset and is therefore the first thing you must do if you intend truly to practise total forgiveness.

You will not let the person who hurt you be afraid of you. Perfect love casts out fear, and fear has to do with punishment (1 John 4:18). When we haven't forgiven we want the person who has hurt us to be intimidated and fearful of us. Many marriages are on the rocks because one keeps the other in fear all the time. By the way, most marriages could be healed overnight if both will stop pointing the finger. Love keeps no record of wrongs (1 Cor. 13:5). Why do we keep records? To prove what happened. So a husband says to his wife, 'I will remember that'. And he is true to his word. Total forgiveness is tearing up the record of wrongs and burning it. Both must do it. For when we have totally forgiven we will not allow people to be afraid of us. God has forgiven us and does not want us to be afraid of him once we are in the family. He gives us the Holy Spirit whereby we cry 'Abba, Father' (Rom. 8:15). No fear there. And there will be no fear when we have forgiven the injustice that has been perpetrated against us. Do not let them fear you!

You will not make them feel guilty. 'I forgive you but I hope you feel bad about what you did.' That is the most normal and natural feeling in the world. That is why I say that total forgiveness is supernatural. When you do not want them even to feel guilty you crossed over a line that separates the natural from the supernatural; you then and there crossed over into the supernatural. God doesn't want us to feel guilty and when we have totally forgiven them we in turn won't send people on a guilt trip when they have hurt us. You may say, 'You don't have to forgive them unless they repent first'. Really? Jesus said, 'Father, forgive them, for they do not know what they are doing' (Luke 23:34). There was not a hint of forgiveness at the cross. Make Jesus your model, not the ancient Law that allows 'tit for tat'. Don't wait for them to be sorry; chances are you will wait until you die. Sadly, most people we have to forgive don't think they have done anything anyway! Don't wait for them. Just forgive them. Do it now. Feel good inside.

You let them save face. You protect their self-esteem. We all have big egos. We love that person who lets us save face, who acts like he or she didn't even know what we did. When we do that to another person, we win a friend for life. God lets *us* save face. He wants us to pass that on to others. Cover for them. Protect them from being exposed. Don't even act like you know what they did to you or 'how great this hurt was'. Total forgiveness is carried out when the person you had to forgive doesn't even know it was a problem for you. We are talking about supernatural grace. By the way, if these lines convict you, don't run to the telephone and call someone to say, 'I forgive you.' Why? They will almost always say, 'For what?' You will say, 'Well, you know.' They will reply, 'Sorry, but I have no idea what you are talking about.' By this time you are getting hot under the collar and you will say, 'Well, you should know!' The result: you have a real fight on your hands! It is a fact – I wish it weren't true – nine out of ten people we have to forgive do not think they have done anything wrong, even if you put them under a lie detector. You must even forgive them for not thinking they have done anything wrong. It is part of letting them save face. The only time we say 'I forgive you' is when they are begging for it and want to hear those comforting words.

You protect them from their deepest hurt. Chances are, you know something about another person that, were you to tell it, would ruin them for life. And if you happen to have knowledge of your enemy that, were it to be known, would ruin them, you have an opportunity to show graciousness. You never – ever – tell what you know. You protect their reputation. We all have skeletons in the cupboard. How would you like it if God decided to pull a skeleton out of your cupboard? But he won't. He isn't like that. We are to be godly – like God. To be merciful as our Father in heaven is merciful (Luke 6:36). And don't be too surprised if the person or people you have to forgive is known to be 'godly'. Have you heard this poem:

Living with the saints above, with those we love, oh, that
  will be glory;
Living with the saints below, with those we know, well,
  that's another story.

Anon

You practise the same total forgiveness as long as you live. I'm sorry,
but it is a life sentence – a life commitment. You don't do it
only once; you do it again tomorrow, and the day after that,
the week after that, the year after that – every day. A husband
says to his wife, 'I thought you said you forgave me.' She
replies: 'That was yesterday.' You have to do it again today.
Sometimes it gets harder, sometimes it gets easier. In either
case, you keep on doing it. Once is not enough. It is for life.
You keep it up. God does! And yet this may be the hardest
part – having to keep forgiving them – long after the event.
This is because the devil will come alongside and remind us
of what they did, how they aren't going to get caught and are
off the hook – and it hurts. This is why we have to keep on
doing it. Total forgiveness never stops. I wish there were a pill
we could take, or a blessing we can receive by the laying on
of hands – or whatever, that will remove the need to keep
forgiving. If only. It ain't easy! You do it every day for the
rest of your life. Even if it gets easy (and it probably will
eventually), you still keep on doing it.

You pray for them. This means you bless them, you pray that
God will bless them. God does not want you to say, 'Lord, I
commit them to you.' That's not the kind of praying he wants
to hear. He wants you to pray for their being blessed, forgiven
and prospered. I remember praying once for a particular
person who had been hurtful to one of our children. I prayed
for this person. It was as though the Lord stopped me and

said, 'Do you mean what you are saying? That you want me to bless this person – to bless and prosper them as if they did no wrong?' It gave me pause. Because I really thought that if I pray that God will bless them he surely won't! But God said to me that if I prayed for him to bless them, he is set free to do just that and would answer my prayer. I had to think hard before I yielded again and said, 'Yes Lord, bless them. Bless them.' But it hurt.

There is an important theological clarification that needs to be stated. We are not saved – or do we become Christians – because of our totally forgiving others, neither are we kept saved by doing this. Otherwise, salvation would be by works. And we know that salvation is by grace, not works. 'For it is by grace you have been saved, through faith – and this not from yourselves, it is the gift of God – not by works, so that no one can boast' (Eph. 2:8-9). This means we are saved by the sheer grace of God. It comes by transferring our trust in our good works to what Jesus did for us on the cross. If you can sing this hymn from your heart, you may be assured of your salvation:

> My hope is built on nothing less than Jesus' blood and righteousness;
> I dare not trust the sweetest frame, but wholly lean on Jesus' Name.
>
> On Christ, the solid Rock, I stand; all other ground is sinking sand.
>
> Edward Mote (1797–1874)

If, however, your hope of salvation and going to Heaven is based upon your works – even your best works, I have to tell you that you are still an unconverted person. I don't mean to be unfair, but anybody who trusts in their works to be saved is not saved and is not a Christian. But if you have put 'all your eggs into one basket', Jesus' death on the cross, do not fear – you are eternally saved.

You can be thankful indeed that total forgiveness is not a condition of salvation; otherwise, would anybody be saved? God knows our frame, he remembers that we are dust (Ps. 103:14). Our Lord Jesus is touched with the feeling of our weaknesses, having been tempted at every point like us – but without sin (Heb. 4:15). He knows that to put total forgiveness as a condition of salvation would be out of reach of any of us. Salvation is by grace through faith – relying on the blood of Jesus to save us.

You will ask, but did not Jesus warn immediately after giving us the Lord's Prayer, 'If you forgive men when they sin against you, your heavenly Father will also forgive you. But if you do not forgive men their sins, your Father will not forgive your sins' (Matt. 6:14)? Yes, and as I say in my treatment of the Lord's Prayer in *Total Forgiveness*, this solely pertains to our *fellowship* with the Father – intimacy with him, which is broken when we do not forgive. The first petition in the Lord's prayer is 'your kingdom come' – a prayer that we would experience the rule of the Father in us. It is the sense of the presence of God one experiences with the ungrieved Holy Spirit. In other words, the continued fellowship with the Father is based upon our walking in the light and the cleansing blood of Jesus is the basis of that fellowship – which *is* conditional (1 John 1:7).

To summarise: salvation is based upon the condition of trusting the blood of Jesus which he shed on the cross; fellowship with the Father is based upon the condition of our walking in the light – which requires total forgiveness.

When I do not forgive, I lose something. Not salvation, but I do lose a sense of God's presence, inner peace and joy and the clear thinking I referred to above. This to me is a fairly strong motivation to forgive! But how wonderful that God doesn't put a pistol to our heads and require such a gracious work by us in order to be saved or to keep saved!

I want to tell you precisely *why* I said that the darkest hour we ever went through was the best thing that ever happened to us. First, it led to a restoration of joy and peace that I myself had lost many years before. I once knew a most unusual peace and sense of the presence of Jesus. There was a time when the person of Jesus was more real to me than anybody around me. Literally. He was that real! But I lost it perhaps a year later. I tried every way under the sun to get that peace back – praying two hours a day (which did me no harm), tithing, double tithing (which did me no harm), having people to pray for me and with me and lay hands on me to transfer more anointing (none of these things did me any harm). But I never got the peace back. It was not until I took Joseph Tson's counsel seriously that I was able to come back to such joy. It did not happen in a second or two; it was a process of weeks and months. I blush to think how bitter I had become and am amazed that God would even use me over the years. Don't tell me God is not gracious – even when we are most unworthy!

Secondly, I used to pray for unction – an archaic word for the anointing. The anointing is the power of the Spirit within that makes things easy. The anointing is the way of ease and least fatigue. It is what enables you to function at a level with which you are comfortable. I wanted it more than anything else in the world. I do not claim to have all the anointing I want, for I yearn for more. But I can say with utter candour that something did happen: more insight than I ever dreamed possible began to flood my mind; a liberty in the pulpit and with people emerged that I had not experienced; and a boldness and fearlessness with regard to my personal reputation brought me into a security within myself that I always wanted. I cannot say that what people think does not matter to me. But I *can* say that what they think doesn't matter much!

Third, my relationship with the Lord has been transformed. It led to my wanting to spend more time with him than ever. It brought me into a sensitivity to the Holy Spirit that revealed exactly *when* I grieve him – and a knowledge that I please him. It enabled me to want to be a better husband, a better father and a better Christian. I can trace it all to that pivotal moment when Joseph Tson said, 'RT, you must *totally forgive* them.'

Julia Fisher, the 'voice' that opens each chapter and who has written each account of total forgiveness, is well known as a broadcaster. But she is a highly gifted writer as well, which you will shortly recognise. She is known by her colleagues as a genuine professional and her voice is very recognisable to listeners of Premier Radio in London. I first asked to meet her after she wrote a review of my book *The Anointing* several years ago which so encouraged me. She invited me to be on Premier Radio with her for a programme, and this kind of invitation was repeated again and again. She then asked me to join her in getting a group of people to go on a tour of Israel and Oberammergau in 2000. If you want to have a good laugh, get someone at Premier to play the unedited tape of our trying to do a commercial to persuade people to come with us to Oberammergau – I could not, even if you paid me ten thousand pounds, pronounce the word correctly for over fifteen minutes. And we were later a part of a group of 250 British Christians in a 'pray for the peace of Israel' tour in 2002. It was because of that very tour and through Julia that I met Canon Andrew White, the Archbishop of Canterbury's envoy to the Middle East, who has given me a surprising ministry to certain leaders in the Middle East.

And now I am going to hand you over to Julia. The next words you read will be hers as she introduces the first beautiful story.

RT Kendall

1

Loss of Innocence
– Agie Ball

To meet Agie Ball is to meet a warm, fun-loving person with a penetrating gaze. When we first sat down to talk, it was over a cup of coffee in our home. Nothing could have prepared me for the story that was to unfold because today Agie is self-assured, extremely articulate and very friendly.

Here you will read her own description of her upbringing – her lack of schooling, being sent to Scotland where she suffered at the hands of an abusive uncle . . . and how in later life she found the key and the ability to forgive. Agie takes up her story:

'My story is not about what others were and did, but about what we are and can do. In my case, it is the revelation of who I am now in Jesus Christ and the deep unveiling of forgiveness and love that has produced a reliable and transformed life. My worth is not based on my past, present or future, but on what Jesus has done: "Before I formed you in the womb I knew and approved of you . . ." (Jer. 1:5, Amplified Bible). Receiving God's love and approval in my life has been the doorway to knowing who I am and what I can do through him.

'Hidden away behind closed doors, many crimes and sins are committed, but sexual abuse to young, innocent children is one of the worst. Invariably it is carried out by someone the child trusts and loves. Sadly, today this is all too familiar.

'From the age of five to ten, over periods of three to six months, my uncle stole many parts of my young formative years; trampled them like young shoots, tender and defenceless. I was left with inexplicable pain that I locked away and chose not to look at or remember. He crippled my ability to trust people and I was bruised with emotion and fear. This left me with very little self-worth. Although I was not responsible for my uncle's actions and evil choices, as I grew up I believed that I was.

'I have discovered that living life without shame starts at the cross of Jesus Christ; this totally destroys the devil's lies and power. All the negative feelings, disappointment, fear and disgrace go. Jeremiah talks about God being Jeremiah's helper and strength, and he told him not to be afraid of the faces of men (Jer. 1:8). With God's help, the past can be as if it has never been.

'Recently, after both my parents died, I felt the freedom to be able to share my story and my walk to forgiveness with my family. One of the most tender and precious experiences came when I felt it was right to share my secret with my four grown-up children and ask their permission to publicly tell my story. It was a surprise and a shock to them to discover that their mother, such a "free" woman, could have experienced "such a past". They all brought positive encouragement and love, but one of my grown-up sons cried and hugged me. He also felt deep anger at the sin that had been imposed on me. It was one of the most precious moments of my life when I experienced that expression of love. Instantly, it reminded me, and gave me a vivid picture, of how God weeps over us and our pain and that he has a righteous anger and hatred of sin.

'As I watched the tears well up in my son's eyes and slowly run down his handsome face, I knew in my heart that my story of Jesus's love and forgiveness was not to be my secret any longer.

'When I got home from school as a child, I can remember feeling sick in my stomach as I banged on the front door. On one occasion I must have been banging for twenty minutes before I got a response. When my mother eventually came to the door, her eyes were fallen and sluggish in her beautiful face, and she was holding on to the side of the door for support. Confusion and fear gripped me as she berated me for being late home. I said, "But you were supposed to come and collect me, and you didn't." Fortunately, the woman who had dropped me home had also invited me to have tea with her daughter, and my mother said I could go. I just wanted to run. I was aware from that moment that life was difficult.

'My mother came from a well-off Christian family; she was one of four girls and six boys. There was an early stage in her life when they were quite poor, but God was at work by teaching them how to be content and fulfilled with very little. My mother had an uncle who had unjustly taken over the family business: a coal merchant's in Rutherglen in Scotland. It was by rights my grandfather's business, and there was a lot of friction between him and this particular uncle, who used to get savagely drunk every Saturday night – that was his form of entertainment. He used to turn up raging, banging on the door where they lived, and they would take him in until the drink had worn off for fear of disturbing the neighbours and causing a nuisance.

'My mother often used to tell me this story, so it had obviously greatly affected her and very likely contributed to her character and the mother she was to me. She used to hide underneath the dining room table when this uncle came in and would stay there motionless beneath the long velvet drapes and tassels, rigid with fear until he had either fallen asleep or left the house. She grew up very nervous and shy because of this regular family event. But she was a very beautiful and lovely woman (and was a little bit spoilt because of this, particularly by my grandmother). She became a very good tailoress, and the family business was later rightfully put back into my grandfather's hands and they began to do very well.

'My mother's family then moved from the very small house in Rutherglen into the countryside and bought a small farm with a most exquisite house. The family was there for several years before my mother's sisters began to marry and leave home. My mother joined the army as a driver to the officers, but while she was doing this job she was raped, twice. This obviously added to her already nervous disposition. She became genuinely frightened of people and, worse still, of life itself. Desperate to help, her mother took her to the doctor to see if he could do something for this nervousness. He prescribed her the drug phenobarbitone. Today, this is a "controlled" drug, usually only given in extreme cases of anxiety or epilepsy and only taken at night.

'My father was an only child, like myself, and came from a modest background. He had lived in Brighton all his life.

His personality was always a happy one and throughout my formative years, and beyond, the atmosphere my father produced was one of humble godliness, and people responded to his unpretentious strengths and energy. Later on in life, I had no problem understanding and identifying with a "heavenly Father" who loved me. My father was gifted in sports and music and played the saxophone; he was also a talented carpenter.

'My parents met in 1944 in Glasgow at the YMCA near to my mother's home and they immediately fell in love. They were married early the following year and decided to set up home in the Brighton area. This was a huge move for my mother who was still very nervous. She later told my father about what had happened to her, but at that stage I do not think he was aware of the severity of her nervousness and anxiety.

'For my mother, it was a move from luxury to a far simpler lifestyle. My father reluctantly returned to the war, leaving my mother to find them somewhere to live; I was born in the following November. My mother spent long periods without my father while he served at sea. Until the age of two, I have slim memories, but I know that I felt secure and loved. My mother told me I was such a comfort to her.

'When my father was discharged, we moved to a flat in Palmera Square, Hove. It had shared central gardens and was close to the sea and shops. I remember being really happy in that home, and I had my first real friend there – she lived in a flat opposite. Our windows faced each other and we would wave and signal that we were going down to the gardens to play.

'During this time, my father found a job with Timothy Whites and Taylors (later bought up by Boots, the chemists).

He was a hard worker and my parents struggled to make ends meet. I often longed for a brother or sister, and there were times when I felt alone, desperately wanting the company of someone more or less my own age as part of our family. I think my parents would have loved more children too, but often said they could not afford to have any more – and they wanted to do the best for me with what they had.

'My mother's spiritual background was Church of Scotland; she had a Christian faith, but it was not alive. In contrast, my father's family attended a Brethren Assembly and he'd had a real experience of God. He searched for a good church for us all to attend and succeeded in finding a Baptist church with a wonderful pastor, Mr Rudman. My mother went only occasionally to the church, but my father took me regularly. It is wonderful how God builds things into your life; as a young child, I was to have a relationship with Jesus that would be a real backbone for things that were to happen later on: "Your eyes saw my unformed substance, and in Your book all the days [of my life] were written before ever they took shape, when as yet there was none of them" (Ps. 139:16, Amplified Bible).

'In the Sunday school, there was an atmosphere of love and tenderness and I sensed Jesus there. Lily Taylor was my teacher. The room smelt musty and we sat on uncomfortable wooden chairs, but I felt so welcome. Even now, I remember the songs I learned there that became so precious:

> Jesus loves me, this I know, for the Bible tells me so.
> Little ones to Him belong, they are weak, but He is
>   strong . . .

Turn your eyes upon Jesus,
look full in His wonderful face,
and the things of earth will grow strangely dim
in the light of His glory and grace.

All the way to Calvary He went for me.

Build on the rock, not the sand.

Wide, wide as the ocean, is my Saviour's love
. . . I am still a child of His care.

'These biblical truths became a part of me and I sang them frequently, so grew up knowing the love of God. My belief in Jesus and his love for me would for ever be the bedrock of winning many battles in my life and seeing Satan totally and utterly defeated. As a child, I was completely unaware that Satan desired to "sift me like grain" (Luke 22:31, Amplified Bible), or that "The thief comes only in order to steal and kill and destroy" (John 10:10, Amplified Bible).

'Although I felt secure and loved, I did begin to notice a difference between myself and other children, particularly at Christmas and Eastertime. Many girls were in new frocks, but I was not. At the age of five, I started at a local school in Hove and it was so different from the love and welcome I had received at the Sunday school. School was like being in prison. I felt no good. I felt rejected. I decided I did not like it.

'By now my mother was spending most of the day on her own and she started to become dependent on phenobarbitone and to drink. She was not able to look after me properly and was hardly aware if I chose not to go to school. At one time I missed school for nearly four weeks, a substantial gap at such a young age. When I returned to school I did not have a clue what the teacher was talking about. After the lesson the teacher promised to help me catch up, but she never did and consequently I never did catch up. I soon realised that I could get away with several weeks of absence before anyone noticed. I used to listen to the radio; it became my friend and tutor. I listened to *Woman's Hour, Mrs Dale's Diary, The Archers* and *Dan Dare*. I was becoming more and more aware of my mother being strange and that my home life was different from other children's home lives.

'Usually, my mother would meet me at the school gates, but on this particular day she did not turn up. Another mother who was a neighbour, and probably aware of my mother's problem, noticed this and took me home with her daughter. On the way back we stopped at a school uniform shop so that this mother could kit out her daughter. I had never seen anything like it! My gymslip had been sent in a brown parcel from my Aunt Jean in Scotland.

'When I got home I had to bang on the front door for a long time before my mother eventually came to open it. Confusion overwhelmed me. I could not understand how my beautiful mother could look so ugly. I had never seen her look or speak like this before, and her behaviour was becoming very unpredictable. That night, I was really glad when my father came home.

'When I was five and a half, we moved again to Hangleton in north Hove. My father thought my mother might be better in a different environment and hoped this would be a new beginning. But unfortunately it was not the answer. The move helped *me* a little because I had a new school to go to and I was happier, but my mother went downhill when I was between the ages of six and nine. At this time, I hardly had a mother at all and, in a sense, was robbed of this part of my childhood. I remember her often slumped over the kitchen table in a pink dressing-gown. She was like this when I left for school and usually like this when I returned. She did not cook for me, but I guess I must have managed to find some food somehow. In the times when she *was* aware, my mother became guilt-ridden and embarrassed.

'One day after school I found her lying unconscious on the hall floor. I managed to drag her into the bedroom and helped her get into bed and called the doctor. I did not really understand what was going on. I knew she had "bad headaches" and was ill. My father, who was often only back from work for the weekends, cooked for me then. He had all the household chores to catch up on and a vegetable patch to maintain. He mainly grew cabbage and potatoes, so that was my staple diet. He did his best for me, but I still felt neglected by him – though looking back now I can see that I was not. He had to spend a lot of time with my mother.

'One day in the gym at school we had to sit in a line. We all had our navy knickers on and bare feet. I noticed that my feet were black with dirt and quickly curled up my toes to hide it. But we were supposed to sit with our legs stretched out and there was nowhere to hide. One girl pointed out my dirty feet and I quickly replied that my shoes had a leak in them. That was my first deliberate lie. In the moments that followed I was to experience painful emotions that began to make me feel neglected, unloved and, worst of all, ashamed. I could live without the designer uniforms, but I did not want to be labelled as "dirty" by other children. As I sat in the line I wondered about other parts of my body that were not as clean as they should be and I was filled with embarrassment. I started to compare other areas of my life with other children.

I did not like what I discovered, so the lies became a pleasant release from the reality of my environment.

'We had friends and neighbours who knew what my mother was like and I realised later that they kept their children away from me. I always felt that there were whispers going on and voices hidden behind hands. By the age of six, I was fetching all the shopping and running all the errands. My mother only answered the door from the upstairs window. My father felt pressurised by my mother's illness and realised I was being neglected. So one day he told me that he might have to find someone else to look after me.

'My father wanted me to stay with my Aunt Jean in Scotland, but for some reason she could not take me, so instead I was sent to another of my mother's sisters, Aunt Jenny, and her husband, Uncle Jimmy. I knew both my aunts very well. My mother's sister Jean had often come to our home at my father's request at times when he had needed extra help with my mother. I was aware that she loved Jesus and I felt spiritually close to her, so I was sad that I was not going to stay with her. But Aunt Jenny was full of fun and played the piano like Winifred Attwell, so I was not altogether sorry that she would be looking after me. The sisters lived in different crofts and cottages in the same lane, so I was able to freely visit my Aunt Jean whenever I chose. My Aunt Jenny had lost all three of her pregnancies to miscarriage and stillbirths. She was incredibly loving and friendly towards me. Uncle Jimmy was also affectionate towards me and made a fuss of me, which I had missed at home.

'But what seemed acceptable fluffing of my hair and "rough and tumble" on the floor soon began to change. One day after lunch when Aunt Jenny was washing up in the kitchen he took me up off the floor and sat me on his knee and kissed me in what seemed, at first, a natural way and he was talking to me. He kissed me again, though, and I was aware it was not right. He had his tongue in my mouth and I felt uncomfortable. He told me to "shhh". He held on to me tightly as I pulled away and tried to get down. Feelings of confusion, disgust and false comfort flooded through my vulnerable emotions.

'This behaviour went on time and again and I was embarrassed, but I could not explain my feelings. I used to dread him coming home at lunchtime and would go out in all kinds of weathers to avoid him. The croft had no hallway – the bedroom and kitchen were straight off the lounge, where I had to sleep. At night, after Aunt Jenny had gone to bed, he used to read a newspaper until she fell asleep. Then he would start touching me and pulling my hand, trying to make me touch him and to put my hand down his trousers. I used to turn away from him, but there was nowhere to run. I felt trapped.

'My heart would sink and my mouth would become dry with fear as I watched my Aunt Jenny lovingly make up the bed for me on the settee. In my mind, bed became a place of dread and fear. I would wonder if that night would be different and he would not bother with me. But in my heart of hearts I knew there was no escape. I tried not to be tired and pretended I did not need to go to bed, thinking I could get out of the inevitable, but my aunt was very attentive (until her head hit the pillow!) and she made sure I had washed, cleaned my teeth and changed for bed. After that, she would tuck me up and kiss me goodnight. I would not see her until the morning. I would often try to fall asleep, thinking that that would put him off, but my anxious state made me so strung up that it was impossible to sleep. I felt pain, I felt sick,

I hated the touch of his skin and the smell of his body odour. All physical contact from him became disgusting and repulsive.

'I could not put the distress into words. I remember thinking that "my father has never done this to me", and I wondered if all men were like that and it was part of growing up. But because my uncle kept telling me to "shhh", I could not speak. I was trapped and frightened by his strength, and all fun, games and relationships froze. Aunt Jenny did not notice. After he left me at night to go to his own bed, I would lie shaking, tears running in streams down my face, longing for my father and his gentle strength. Who could I tell? Who could help me? My uncle's commands to "be quiet" were deeply embedded in me and I was afraid. Their golden spaniel, Hazel, would lie in front of the ebbing fire and sigh deeply. Hazel was my friend. I often thought she too was relieved when he had gone to bed.

'I would lie and watch the cinders of the fire change colour as they lost their heat and would try to make imaginary pictures out of all the shapes. In my heart I was quietly singing, "Jesus loves me, this I know, for the Bible tells me so. Little ones to Him belong, they are weak, but He is strong."

'One day, my aunt said that my mother was coming. But by then I had changed from being a vivacious little girl into a very introverted one. I was suddenly very quiet and thoughtful and spent much of my time daydreaming. We met my mother in my uncle's car. I was sat in the front with him, and my aunt and mother sat in the back. I looked at her and blanked her. I was unable to kiss or talk to her. She asked me what was wrong, in front of everyone, because I was so obviously ignoring her. I did not want to speak. It was as though there was a fence around me. At the same time, I longed to hug her and snuggle close. I realise now that I was protecting myself from being hurt again, but my heart was crying out for genuine wholesome affection and love.

'My mother had apparently recovered and I went home with her, but soon the process began again. I had such fear in my heart when I was told that I was going to Scotland for the second time. But off I had to go alone. This time, I went to school, but I remained an isolated child. I would often visit my Aunt Jean up the lane, but if I heard my uncle's car coming I would quickly hide in the verge, even if it meant jumping into a bed of stinging nettles.

'I tried where possible to stay away from their home during the day and return at night as late as I was allowed. My Aunt Jenny would often ask me why I had been away so long and if she had upset me. I think she was also noticing how quiet I had become.

'My cunning uncle bought me a pony as a "carrot", and I called her Peggy. She was a bit stubborn, but she was a dream to me, and my uncle knew it gave me a reason to want to stay with them. One day he told me that Peggy needed new shoes and that we must take her to his brother's house, which sounded a reasonable suggestion. Usually, when we approached his brother's house, the Alsatian dog, which was a fearsome guard dog, would begin to bark ferociously, but this time there was silence. No one was home.

'My uncle took me into a barn that seemed to have been prepared for my arrival. I remember feeling sick and needing the toilet. I wanted the ground to swallow me up. He made me stand on a box and I remember trying to push him away, shouting and screaming because of what he wanted to do to me at a height he could manage. I was miles from anyone. It was the most awful experience imaginable; the kind you would like to forget for ever. In my heart I prayed a child's desperate prayer: "Jesus! Help!" It is amazing how God uses the simplest things to confound and send the devil running. This giant was about to fall. God was with me, and I frightened my uncle with my screaming. I suddenly recalled my mum saying to me when I was a small girl that if a strange man ever tried to grab you, you had to scream at the top of your voice. I took the deepest breath and gave it all I had. When I looked at his eyes, this time he was the frightened one. Even though the neighbours were far off, my uncle said, "Let's forget this." So I got on my pony and rode off on my own. In my heart, I was still screaming, but there was definitely an awesome presence in the barn that had protected me.

'The next visit to Scotland was the last one on my own. I was almost ten. Now that I was older and, sadly, rather rebellious, my uncle was beginning to live with the fear of his actions. After the last visit and incident, I think he began to fear reaction and suspicion. But he would still come to me each night. I think because my aunt worked so hard, she went out like a light when she went to bed. He seemed to feel safe in what he was doing.

'One day he took me into a cow shed and pushed a pitchfork under my chin and referred to "our secret". I remember thinking "I'm not part of this". He warned me not to tell and said if I did, my aunt would be put in prison. He knew she offered his only "security"; she would also have to suffer his punishment, and he told me they might lock me up too. As I felt the prongs of the fork in my neck and chin, a sudden relief flooded my stomach. I thought, "Now *he* is afraid." I believed what he said. I loved my aunt and she had done no wrong; I could not bear to think that

I might lose her. Also, "our secret" had got to me and I dreaded the shame and sense of guilt I would feel if anything were made public.

'My mother recovered, then lapsed again, so this time my father sent both my mother and me to Scotland to be looked after. By now, my mother had been given two weeks to live. She was in such a sorry state. Her family found her a good doctor who helped her enormously, but really he was ignorant of her real state. She and I shared a room in Scotland and I was with her when she went "cold turkey". It was horrendous. She was screaming and shaking in the middle of the night. I remember her grabbing hold of me and telling me to run for my life. However, yet again she recovered and we returned to Hove.

'The change in my mother was enormous. She had touched rock bottom and knew that this time it was "make or break". I could tell that not only had her determination been renewed by doctors and family, but she had a new faith in God and a joy in living.

'The day that we returned to our small flat in Hangleton there was such a welcome from my dear father. I knew that for the first time in many years we were going to function as a family. Apart from hugging and loving one another, there was a joy that only comes from the presence of the Holy Spirit.

'As evening approached and I went to *my* room, and *my* bed, what joy! My father had bought new bed linen for me and made up my bed so beautifully. He had put a hot-water bottle in it for me. As I lay between the sheets and felt the gentle warmth, a sense of security and peace washed through me. I felt safe, no one could get at me. Little did my father know how much he had done for me.

'In my mid-teens, a neighbour who had a daughter who was my age asked my parents if I could go with their daughter to church, as they were concerned about her waywardness. This was agreed and we went along to Holland Road Baptist Church where I had gone as a small child. Here I searched for the Jesus I had known as a youngster. There was a wonderful atmosphere there and I could feel God's presence. We also went along to some Sunday after-evening service "squashes", and on one occasion a man called Philip Vogel spoke about the time when Jesus was choosing his disciples and asking them to follow him. I heard how Jesus chose men with dirty hands who were used to hard work. This spoke so strongly to me that I gave my life to the Lord. After that, my life changed so radically that it was as if I had had a brain transplant – suddenly I was able to concentrate well at school. I knew God had met me in a big way and he blessed me with wonderful friendships in that church. There was a real positive love and I knew I could trust it. The pastor was still the same; he was a wonderful "spiritual father" to all his flock – but particularly to the young people. God's Holy Spirit became part of my life, and gradually as I learned to trust his guiding completely, my life changed radically in God's hands.

'My mother changed too at this time. I think she was frightened she might lose me, as I was growing up and changing physically and now old enough to realise and understand more about her. Through prayer, especially on my father's part and through my mother starting to go to work, she improved a great deal.

'In my early twenties, I met my husband-to-be, Philip, through the young people's fellowship at the church. We were married and moved to a house in Scaynes Hill. Philip was a pilot for British Airways and he was often away, leaving me on my own. But my background had given me a thorough schooling for this. I was not fearful about getting married because I had realised that my father was a righteous man and that there were really only one or two odd ones about. Philip loved me and gave me confidence, and my shyness and embarrassment disappeared as I trusted his belief in me. And God was always close, and spoke many important truths to me at that time from Isaiah:

> When you pass through the waters, I will be with you,
> and through the rivers, they will not overwhelm you.
> When you walk through the fire, you will not be
> burned or scorched (Isa. 43:2, Amplified Bible).

'This verse starts off with "When you pass through . . ." That means you come out the other side! The journey of life that followed has for me been one of knowing the presence of God every step of the way. There have been many deep waters, many sprawling rivers and the heat of flaming fires. But God is true to his promise: we have not been overwhelmed or scorched to the extent that we are still dripping wet or carrying the lingering smell of the smoke. There is a freshness in each day through knowing his promise: "I will be with you."

'It was not until I had my own children that God began to deal with my past and with me. When I had my first baby, Daniel, I adored him – as all mothers do with their first – and when I was expecting my second I wondered how I would love my new baby as much. This was when my awareness grew of the lack of love that my mother had shown me and I became bitter and had an unforgiving spirit. I blamed her for not caring for me as a child. I could not understand why drugs and drink had been her first love rather than my father and me. These feelings began to plague me, eat me up, and destroy God's work in my life.

'I knew I had to come to terms with my past and be set free. I knew that I had an Almighty God, that he was King of kings. He could deal with my puny little life. I knew from those childhood songs that his love for me was deep, and that he died for me and could bring me to a place of light in his presence.

'Then one lunchtime, when my two children were having their nap, I sat looking across the fields from one of the bedrooms in our house. I began to confess everything, because although I had been abused, Satan's lie made me feel the guilty party and I needed to confess everything in order to be liberated. My confession was not for God, it was for me. I knew that my mighty God wanted to change my life radically so that I could live in total freedom. When I had finished praying, I asked him to show me that he had heard me and I opened the Bible at 1 Kings 9:3:

> The Lord told him, 'I have heard your prayer and supplication which you have made before Me; I have hallowed this house which you have built, and I have put My Name [and My Presence] there forever. My eyes and My heart shall be there perpetually' (1 Kgs. 9:3, Amplified Bible).

'I would have eaten this scripture if someone had told me to! It was real food for me at that moment in my life. I knew without doubt that God wants to invade our homes and our lives and that he really is the same yesterday, today and for ever. But as I came down the stairs, I started to doubt what had just happened. Then the doorbell rang, and a man stood there who my husband and I had led to the Lord a few years previously. As soon as he saw me, he said to me, "Agie, you've just been with God, haven't you?" He said that my face shone. Well, that was God's seal. God had spoken to me and reassured me as well.

'After that, every day became a new expression of freedom. The foundational lesson that the Holy Spirit was teaching me was about living the life of freedom through faith in Jesus and his word:

> In [this] freedom Christ has made us free [and completely liberated us]; stand fast then and do not be hampered and held ensnared and submit again to a yoke of slavery [which you have once put off] (Gal. 5:1, Amplified Bible).

'This truth began the real path of forgiveness that was so necessary to remain in my new-found freedom. That afternoon I had forgiven my uncle and my mother out of desperation and obedience. Jesus, though, knew forgiveness and restoration are so important for our spiritual well-being that he taught his disciples how to pray about these things:

> And forgive us our debts, as we also have forgiven [left, remitted, and let go of the debts, and have given up resentment against] our debtors (Matt. 6:12, Amplified Bible).

'God told us to do this – I knew there were no options! Throughout my Christian walk I've had to face daily choices, and one of Satan's destructive lies is to tell us that forgiveness does not really matter, that we will get over it, or that time is a great healer!

'Sometimes, I wonder if the pain of the situation we experience keeps us from forgiving – we think that not forgiving is somehow protecting us from the same thing happening again, or future disappointment. I have come to the conclusion that that is a lie! By not forgiving quickly and completely, we first disobey God, and secondly, determine our own forgiveness from the Father:

> For if you forgive people their trespasses [their reckless and wilful sins, leaving them, letting them go, and giving up resentment], your heavenly Father will also forgive you. But if you do not forgive others their trespasses [their reckless and wilful sins, leaving them, letting them go, and giving up resentment], neither will your Father forgive your trespasses (Matt. 6:14–15, Amplified Bible).

'I like the Amplified Version of Matthew, because it talks there of giving up resentment. I knew I had to forgive, but dealing with and letting go of the resentment was a work that took place in my heart. God's Spirit started dealing with my life and these painful issues when my own daughter was just two and a half. Each stage of her growth was a colourful memory of the milestones of my abuse. I protected her with every part of my being. I was so grateful to God that she would be able to experience a safe childhood and enjoy it to the full. I loved her as a precious gift from God, as I did all our children.

'The Spirit of God began to separate my genuine forgiveness towards my uncle and mother from the very real awareness of resentment. This was a painful truth for me because I knew I would have to face issues that, until now, I thought

I could "live with". The depth of forgiveness God was after was perfection, without stain or blemish. His extravagant love for me desired only his standard of life – completely free from hang-ups. The forgiveness, if I dare say it, was almost easy because I obeyed. But I knew I had resentment that I needed to deal with through the following years. Rather like an onion, the layers would gradually be taken off, sometimes with tears of sadness, but mostly joy. One resentment was the snare of daydreaming and make-believe. I was happy to lose myself in this world of counterfeit; the pain of sexual abuse had driven me there. But I learned that this was an escape from reality and a place of protection, and the consequences of this behaviour had already contributed to my poor education.

'I can remember, even today, the times I would gaze out of my classroom window – completely in a world of my own, only to "come to" at the sound of the school bell! The lesson was over and I had missed it. As I grew up, I blamed this escapism and the deprived result on the sexual abuse and thought "why me?" I always felt fulfilled in Jesus, but from time to time the "what ifs" would knock at my door. I would look at other people with qualifications, and what I thought were good jobs, and wished I had had the encouragement and incentives as a child to be an achiever. I know I felt shame at this time, and a painful embarrassment would grip me. I felt different and I disliked myself.

'Graciously the Spirit of God brought me to a place of thorough repentance. I recognised that I felt dissatisfied with what I was, but who was I to object to the road God had mapped out for me? The Spirit lovingly reminded me that it was normal to think these things. God had not finished with me:

> The Lord will perfect that which concerns me; Your
> mercy and loving-kindness, O Lord, endure forever –
> forsake not the works of Your own hands (Ps. 138:8,
> Amplified Bible).

'Thinking back to my teens when God had spoken to me so
much from Isaiah, I knew he had chosen me. With these
great truths being part of me, and the Holy Spirit bringing
them alive, I came to a place of accepting the path I had
walked and the person it had made me:

> For I will pour water upon him who is thirsty, and
> floods upon the dry ground. I will pour My Spirit upon
> your offspring, and My blessing upon your descendants
> (Isa. 44:3, Amplified Bible).

> Shake yourself from the dust; arise, sit [erect in a
> dignified place], O Jerusalem; loose yourself from the
> bonds of your neck, O captive daughter of Zion
> (Isa. 52:2, Amplified Bible).

'I was a product of my life's experiences, but I was able to
genuinely thank God and ask for his forgiveness for not
accepting this and for wishing that I had the gifts of my
friends and peers. I forgave my uncle and my mother in this
particular area, even though it was only a product of the
abuse. It had been a yoke of slavery that had to come off. I
was thirsty to get this forgiveness thoroughly dealt with. Any
dry place in my life where the dirt or consequences of the
abuse had settled and dried hard needed floods of water from
the Holy Spirit. As I accepted the place and will of God in
my life, true forgiveness took away all the bitterness. I really
was able to shake myself from the dust and sit erect, in a

dignified place. It is one of the most precious positions as a daughter of the King, to hold your head up, to be in a place of dignity, because of what Jesus has done:

For God selected [deliberately chose] what in the world is foolish to put the wise to shame, and what the world calls weak to put the strong to shame (1 Cor. 1:27, Amplified Bible).

So then, as it is written, Let him who boasts and proudly rejoices and glories, boast and proudly rejoice and glory in the Lord (1 Cor. 1:31, Amplified Bible).

'Because I was willing for the scrutinising word of God to deal with my heart, my relationship with Jesus was becoming deeper, and the awareness of his Holy Spirit controlling and guiding my life was, and still is, most important. I am proud to boast and rejoice that Jesus wants to do a thorough work in my life. The letting go of what I thought of myself, the shame and sense of failure, was immediately replaced with a secure, purpose-built life that he would use.

'As I write this today I now know that the knowledge and wisdom we can have as a gift from God is to be desired far more than any worldly qualification. Being equipped with truth and understanding from the word of God is an incredible tool in our lives. It has enabled me to live my life by the "maker's instructions", which in turn has produced a life of excellence and God's favour. I am so grateful that I can boast in the knowledge of God's word and not my own achievements.

'I only told my husband about the sexual abuse when we had been married for about five years. Until that time I had never felt the need to. As we were one flesh, I wanted to share what God had been doing in my life. I knew my husband loved me and I did not fear rejection from him in any way. His response was kind and compassionate, and he was most interested in what God had done and the release it had brought in different areas of my life. As we both shared our deepest secrets, it brought us closer together and to the love of Jesus.

'As God continued to deal with my heart, I knew that one day God would provide a moment when I would be able to tell my mother what had happened to me. In God's timing and perfect plan, I was to hold "that secret" for another seventeen years. For now, though, I just had to show her how much I loved her. The forgiveness that God enabled me to release to my mother was massive and an incredible remedy for pain. God allowed this to happen in the complete privacy of my heart.

'But even in those early days I knew that I would never tell my father. I felt it would destroy him, and that the sadness would be more than he could bear. I realised I needed to be sensitive to his strengths and weaknesses, especially in revealing something so intense and painful. My father was not a weak man, but his desire was to please God and walk in righteousness. This sin would have been too much for him to bear. He had had enough pain watching my mother in her worst days, and the continuing responsibility of me weighed heavily upon him.

'At this stage of my mother's life, she was so much better. She never became totally free from the drug that had stolen so much of life and happiness from our family, but now she seemed to manage the drug instead of it controlling her. She was fun to be with, her personality was reliable, and her love and generosity were extravagant and gracious to all of us.

Both my parents adored their grandchildren and came to our home often, so we enjoyed many happy days together. During these times I was able to work out my forgiving spirit towards my mother without mentioning the word "forgiveness" once.

'There were many days of opportunity with my mother. I would watch how she would play with the children, speak kind words to them, and advise them with a godly wisdom that one does not acquire overnight! Her love for them was intense but not overwhelming, and I could sense how the children loved her and appreciated their grandparents being around. I could not help but wish she had been like that with me: the way she bathed them, folded their clothes, wiped their noses, or took them to the toilet.

'I felt she was trying to make up for what she had not given me as a little girl – and somehow in loving my children she was loving me. She would frequently encourage and tell me "what a good mother" I was. In my heart I knew she was blaming herself and was so very sorry for neglecting me. I would often reassure her of my love. My forgiveness of the past ensured that we had a future together, a relationship that grew deeper and richer all the time. I was determined that nothing would hamper what God was building.

'This new closeness and quality mothering I was experiencing in later life was a joy. God was good. I had my mother back, and a very precious grandmother for my children. I know that if I had not come to that place of real forgiveness, I would have held our relationship at a distance. We could have missed out on so much.

'As my older daughter reached the age of six, I often had flashbacks of how I would have been during those intimidating painful years. Looking at her, I saw how beautifully God's creative and artistic hand had made her with such innocence and purity. She was always keen to learn and do well at everything she put her hand to, and she had a spiritual understanding beyond her years. Every stage of her life gave me great joy; she grew up to be my friend and a real rock in times of trouble. The generations are now being blessed and favoured as God promised.

'During those early years of her life, silly little things would cause my memories to churn up pain. As she would put on clean white socks and a freshly laundered uniform on Mondays and be reasonably happy to go to school, I would remember how I would hide behind our curtains watching children who lived close by, walking to school with their mums. I would remember how my hair would never be brushed and the plaits would eventually fall out on their own. I would go back into our little kitchen and check my mother had not fallen off her chair where she slouched over the table. My daughter's little body was so perfectly formed, her mouth and eyes so innocent to the things of the world. I would look at her and feel the memories of the pain and wonder if my uncle was really an animal. How could he have done what he did to me? Where was his respect for human beings? Did he have no sense of protection towards an innocent child? I felt sick, and my anger turned to intense dislike and hatred of this man.

'The memories were very real and the flashbacks caused physical discomfort and pain. I knew that Satan was trying to take ground that he had lost when I had forgiven my uncle. I remembered the warning – to not be ensnared by a yoke of slavery. I had to stand fast and believe and proclaim God's promise. But at this time God was probably doing the deepest work of all in my heart. My mother had been easy to love because she was "lovable". I had thought that the obedience in forgiving my uncle for the sin he committed on my body and life was enough, but I began to realise that when we really *love* the sinner, as Jesus did, then Satan has completely and utterly lost the battle.

'I cried to Jesus to give me this supernatural love for my uncle, so that I would begin to see him as Jesus saw him when he died on the cross for my uncle's life. I prayed and prayed for this, until I knew it had become part of me and it was genuine. Eventually with a heart of forgiveness firmly established, I was able to pray for him with God's love, and asked the God whom I trust to bless him and bring him to a place of repentance for his own sake. The forgiveness was complete. The sting had completely gone from the memories of the past and I was even able to remember the happy times without any fear. I know of no other love than the love of Jesus that could do such a complete melting of the hatred that was in my heart. The curse was turned to blessing! I realised that forgiveness does not always mean a restoration of relationship. We have to be wise as to where the other person stands in the situation, especially with regard to abuse. But there was a peaceful acceptance that the past really was behind me.

'The years went by, and tragically a cousin of mine had a fatal farming accident at the age of twenty-one. My mother and I went together to the funeral which was in Scotland. Ripples of fear tried to spoil my life again, a visit to Scotland! Even though there was a very real sad reason for going, I started to wonder how I would cope with familiar territory and mixed memories and meeting my uncle again. But the reassurance from God's Spirit was amazing; I felt strong and knew I would be a support to my mother.

'It was a sad day. Together, as the larger family, we

remembered the life of this young man, and after the service we all went to his parents' home for refreshments. It was a joy to see uncles, aunts and cousins, and yes, my uncle was there too. I spoke to him briefly after shaking his hand (it was a big thing for me to touch him), and at that moment the realisation of just how much Jesus had healed me and set me free came streaming through all the anticipated fear of the occasion. I felt it was godly to be polite, but I did not encourage any deep or prolonged conversation; besides, I had many loved ones I wanted to catch up with. The cousin who had died had a beautiful sister and she was a great help to her mother as she hosted the afternoon and made sure that everyone had enough food and drink. But I noticed something in her behaviour and actions towards our uncle. She definitely avoided him and yet was graciously friendly to everyone else. I identified with her actions.

'After my mother and I had returned home, we spent a day together. We were recalling our trip and the mixture of joy and sadness. She started to ask me if I had noticed how cold and snooty my cousin had been at the wake, particularly to my uncle. My mum went on and on about her attitude and really ran her down. Something rose up in me in defence of this young woman and I found myself saying – "Maybe she was protecting herself." From then on, the comments became intense questions, and my responses more difficult to answer truthfully.

'I loved my mother far too much to cause her any pain, but my mother's conclusion that this man could do no wrong really riled me. She was talking about the man who through selfish sin could have ruined my life, had it not been for the power of God. Then to back up my initial suggestion, I found myself saying, "Maybe what happened to me happened to her as well." Strangely, deep inside, I felt my mother knew immediately what I was talking about.

'The questions flowed like torrents, and I found I had the strength to truthfully answer in depth and in detail. Her reaction at first was one of horror and disgust. Then came her guilt, sadness and tears of remorse – ultimately she was blaming herself. We spent a very painful – but beautiful – afternoon together. I knew that this was the moment God's Spirit had promised me seventeen years earlier. With God's help and sensitivity I was determined that together we would break every remaining hold that Satan had on either of us.

'My mother found it hard to believe that I had kept my secret for all those years from everyone but my husband. I insisted that she also told no one, especially not my father, or my mother's sister Jenny: two people that I greatly loved. Aunt Jenny had replaced the love and care that my mother and father were unable to give me at certain stages of my life, and she had treated me like her own. I thought if she were told about the abuse, she would "lose" the husband she believed she had. Some things you have to leave entirely to God. Looking back, I cherish the memories of what happened that afternoon. As we sat in the kitchen, our hearts bursting, and tears flowing, all the remorse and sorrow that had clung on to my mother let go.

'The anger and hatred my mother had for my uncle gushed out, the floodgates were wide open, and I was now in an explosive situation. I could see that the result of this guilt was being transferred into anger and blame towards my uncle. The stages of shock, remorse, sadness, vexation, guilt, and now this attributed blame, were hard to handle. I felt as if I were walking on a tightrope. In the moments that followed I realised why God's Spirit had done such a thorough work in my life and how perfect the stages of forgiveness had been. That day, I was presented with the opportunity to complete my tragic story with a glorious ending!

'With great love and patience we worked through every area of pain my mother had felt that afternoon. I was able to tell her how I had taken to Jesus my sadness and confusion about the lack of mothering I felt I had received. How I had spoken out my sense of worthlessness and failure and how frightened I was to be myself. I explained how God had met me, and confirmed through his word that he had heard my cry and my prayer. How the forgiveness was dealt with and about the amazing way he had renewed my love for her. I told her how much I valued her, what she meant to me, and how in the worst situations of my past I had never stopped loving her.

'Even in these painful but joyous moments God was building a deeper, permanent love. We spoke of her own forgiveness towards herself, and ultimately towards my uncle. She spent many occasions after that talking to "her maker", coming to terms with her past life, and the feelings of remorse and hatred. The vexation and grief she felt took time to be replaced with God's solutions. She told me her heart was in the process of being melted and reformed in the hands of God. I knew what she meant. The comfort we were to one another that day, and the years that followed, was a real gift:

And I will restore or replace for you the years that the locust has eaten – the hopping locust, the stripping locust, and the crawling locust, My great army which I set among you. And you shall eat in plenty and be satisfied and praise the name of the Lord, your God,

Who has dealt wondrously with you. And My people
shall never be put to shame (Joel 2:25–6, Amplified Bible).

'I knew the final blow came to Satan when I told my mother
I loved her and *forgave* her. We had a brand-new start together
and wanted to make the most of it. My freedom was complete;
Christ had indeed made me *free*. I had put away the past and
had let it go.

'As a family we have experienced the favour of God, for
he has been so generous to us. My husband and I came from
very poor and restricted beginnings and we have both learnt
the lessons of being content with what we have. Now in
these better times the example of generosity from God and
our parents flows into every area of our life. "The Rock" I
learned to build my life upon as a little girl singing Sunday
school songs is still standing today, totally reliable, firm and
strong.

'My parents continued to live full, happy, godly lives until
they died in their eighties. They served the Lord with an
example of godly righteousness and generosity that was an
example to our family and beyond. The greatest tribute I
could ever pay to such dear parents is to say that they did
not leave trinkets, but a legacy of love and conscientious
commitment to God and their family, which in turn I now
see being worked out in my grandchildren. My mother died
first and I was able to be with her a few days before her death.
I took her hand, and we looked intensely into one another's
eyes, and I said, "Oh, I do love you, Mum." Struggling for
breath, she replied, "And I've always loved you."

'Forgiveness allowed me never again to carry a spirit of
heaviness and shame. The curse of sin had become a blessing.
Now, only God can do that!'

True Love

Jesus I need to know true love
Deeper than the love found on earth
Take me into the King's chamber
Cause my love to mature

Let me know the kisses of your mouth
Let me feel your warm embrace
Let me smell the fragrance of your touch
Let me see your lovely face

Take me away with you
Even so, Lord, come
I love you Lord
I love you more than life

My heart and my flesh yearn for you, Lord
To love you is all I can do
You have become my sole passion
Cause my love to be true

David Ruis,
Mercy/Vineyard Publishing, 1994

(All Bible references in this chapter are taken from the Amplified Bible, published by the Zondervan Corporation and the Lockman Foundation 1987.)

2

I Married a Black Man
– Kate Jinadu

I first heard about Kate Jinadu while working on a programme for Premier Radio. She sent me a letter to say she was about to visit Ibadan, Nigeria, where she was organising a large 'empowerment' conference for women to be held in an amusement park. I remember being intrigued by her name; Kate sounded so English, while Jinadu sounded so Nigerian! Curious to find out more about this lady, I called her and arranged a radio interview. When we met, sure enough, she was 100 per cent English! However, over thirty years ago, Kate married a Nigerian man. That wedding provides the backdrop to this story, because Kate was to discover, to her deep sorrow, that for a white girl to marry a black man was unacceptable to her family. That such attitudes could exist might sound strange today. But we have to remember that the face of British society has changed enormously in a generation. Today, we are a cosmopolitan society, and to visit London is to visit a city where over a hundred languages are spoken! But forty years ago, things were very different and it was unusual to see

*a black person, especially outside of our large cities – and it was
almost unheard of for a white person to marry a black person. And so
it is into this racially sensitive situation that Kate's story is set. Kate
takes up the tale:*

' "You are a wicked and ungrateful girl. You are destroying
this family. Look what you are doing to your poor mother."
The speaker was my aunt – "She Who Must Be Obeyed".
She was only four feet eleven inches tall, but was nevertheless
a formidable lady with a powerful tongue.

'What she said appeared to be true. My mother was
extremely distressed and had taken to her bed. My father was
deeply unhappy too. "We were always so proud of you," he
told me mournfully. The rest of the sentence, not yet spoken,
hung in the air between us, ". . . now we're ashamed of you
and your behaviour is highly embarrassing."

'At the Bible College where I was a student there had
been another violent reaction. Again I was told that I was
misguided and misinformed. "Satan is appearing as an angel
of light" was the comment of the Dean of Women. In addition,
a well-known prayer warrior wrote to me that my behaviour
was totally unacceptable and that she was praying against this
"project" every day. Even my closest friend at college had
told me, "Wow, Kate, you're very brave. I couldn't do it!"

'And the cause of the controversy? I wanted to marry.
Who did I want to marry? An African, but not a white African;
that would have been fine. My husband-to-be was black. In
contrast, I am not black!

'My aunt was still speaking. I studied the floor, eyes
downcast, saying nothing. What more could I say? We had
been going round the same arguments for over a year now.
We'd held family meetings with my pastor, talking endlessly,

getting nowhere. We had reached an impasse. As my aunt continued talking I was suddenly hit with a bolt of pure joy. It seemed to enter through my head and suffuse my whole being. I wanted to leap, to dance, and to shout. I wanted to burst out laughing. I wanted to run round the house shouting, "I'm getting married, I'm getting married. Celebrate!"

'Some words from the Bible that Jesus himself had spoken suddenly came into my mind: "Blessed are you when people insult you, persecute you and falsely say all kinds of evil against you because of me. Rejoice and be glad, because great is your reward in heaven, for in the same way they persecuted the prophets who were before you" (Matt. 5:11–12).

'Marriage was something every woman longed for, but here I was being made to feel ashamed, unclean and dishonourable. "Lord," I prayed, "Help me not to laugh out loud!"

'Later, in my room, I knelt down to thank him. The joy was still there, bubbling and effervescing through me. "Lord, thank you for your blessing and for your understanding. This marriage was your idea. I would never have thought of marrying a black African. It would not have entered my (tiny) mind. Give me the courage to go on and the grace to forgive."

'The year was 1966, and the conversation (monologue!) with my aunt, and God's response, is a moment I will never forget. The infusion of God's favour was (dare I say it?) similar to the experience of the young Mary when she responded to the angel, "I am the Lord's servant. May it be to me as you have said" (Luke 1:38).

'I was walking through an experience with God and I was entirely alone. My fiancé (I couldn't even call him that since we were not officially engaged) was 200 miles away in Scotland working with the Faith Mission. I had once been a rebel but now, having given my life unreservedly to God some four years earlier, I genuinely wanted not only to please him and bring him joy, but also to obey my parents, my mentors at college, and anyone else who cared to "speak into my life". Now, in obeying God, my behaviour was causing grief, outrage and distress. Maybe I should abandon the project and stay single.

'Paradoxically, the issue of singleness was one I had already dealt with. When I enrolled in the Bible College of Wales I was twenty-four, a virgin, and looking for a future marriage partner. What better place to find someone of like mind than at a Bible School? I couldn't wait to meet all those wonderful men. I had kept myself pure and now I was awaiting God's reward – a handsome hunk and the father for our future children!

'The college had strict rules. Apart from lectures and prayer meetings (every night!), male and female students were strictly segregated and socialising and fraternisation were not allowed. However, human nature being what it is – the allure of the unattainable – many students from the college went on to marry one another on leaving, and among the fraternity it was jokingly known as "The Bridal College of Wales"!

'My aspirations, though, were soon to be shattered. First, as I conducted my survey, I discovered there was no one I found appealing. Well, there was *one* who seemed to me to be head and shoulders above the rest, but he was the wrong colour . . . so I gave him no further thought. His name was Paul Jinadu, a Muslim who had converted to Christianity. The year was 1963. Black/white mixed marriages were unheard of – well, almost. I had heard of *one*, and that was actually in Africa, which, as far as I was concerned, could have been a million miles away.

'But that was not all. During my second month at college in Wales we studied the life of Abraham. We were considering his willingness to sacrifice his only son – the son of promise, Isaac. We read of their three-day journey into the wilderness and how Abraham had tied his son to the altar and taken a knife to slaughter him. "God can ask us to be prepared to do some very bizarre things," Dr Symonds was saying. "Maybe he will ask some sacrifice of you."

'I felt very smug. Surely I had sacrificed enough. I had left secure employment, given away all my money (it wasn't much); I had even given away my jewellery and expensive clothes. I had deigned to come to this little-known establishment rather than Bristol University as my father had wished. I had chosen not to take the government grant offered to all students, but rather to pray to my Father in secret that he might reward me openly. In other words, I trusted God to supply my fees and all my other needs. At that very moment, my pressing need was toothpaste! Sacrifice? I gave myself ten out of ten!

' "What is the thing most precious to you?" Dr Symonds continued. "What do you desire above all else?"

' "Marriage and children," I muttered to myself.

' "Supposing he is asking you to surrender these things to him. What would you do?"

'I was aghast. It was outrageous. God would *never* ask such a thing of me – would he?

' "That's not fair, Father," I protested. "You know how you made me. I'm made for marriage. I've got hormones. I *love* children."

'There was nothing. Silence. Zilch. I was in shock.

'It seemed that the question of marriage and my willingness to abandon the idea was exactly what he *was* asking. For seven days I was in turmoil. I could not sleep. I had no peace. I almost felt as if God had betrayed me. What I was being asked was beyond me. A visiting speaker helped me out. "When God asks you to do something you feel you simply cannot do, try praying the prayer: 'Father, make me willing to be willing.' "

'I had been thrown a lifeline and I took it: "Father, make me willing to be willing to be single and celibate."

'I had done it! I was free! Peace returned and I felt a real sense of joy and relief. I would never marry. Well, so be it.

'I struck men off my agenda and began to seek a deeper walk with the Holy Spirit. One of the things I prayed during this time was, "Lord, show me my heart." When he responded I almost wished that I had not made such a request. I thought my heart was fairly OK. After all, I didn't lie – well, not often. I didn't cheat or swear – well, only if pushed. I didn't gossip – well, not a lot. So although once I had been a rebel, surely now I was fairly respectable? Unfortunately for me, that was not how God viewed my heart.

'I read in the Bible, "The heart is deceitful and desperately wicked; who can know it?" I certainly did not know mine. When God showed me my heart I saw that I was full of pride and arrogance, including racial pride. He reminded me that he resists the proud but gives grace to the humble, and that pride is the sin he hates above *all* others. Humility was a concept entirely foreign to me. He also showed me that my heart held the seeds of every sin imaginable; only a loving stable background and parental protection had sheltered me. I was appalled as I viewed my heart through God's pure eyes, and when it was over I felt like St Paul when he described himself as "the chief of sinners".

'This realisation greatly helped me in my assessment of

others. If I was so great a sinner now cleansed and forgiven by God, what right had I to judge or condemn any other individual? None.

'Exactly nine months later, Paul Jinadu asked me to marry him.

'I had finished my first year at the college and Paul, who was a year ahead of me, had completed the course and left. We were not particularly friendly, but I felt sad that I would never see him again. But during my holiday I was invited to take part in a mission, and there he was! I did not know that he would be part of the team, so it was an unexpected pleasure to be working with him. On the fourth day of the mission we had a half-day break. I was eager to learn more about the Holy Spirit as there were so many things I didn't understand. I had a long list of questions to ask, and Paul patiently talked me through them. I was really happy and got up to go.

' "Now I have a question for you," he said.

'I felt impatient. "What is it?"

' "Will you marry me?"

'I was utterly astonished. A tornado of confusion tore through my mind. Is he serious? I hardly know him. If he were so spiritual, he would know I'm not getting married. How could he make such a massive mistake? Does he think he's white? Doesn't he know that black and white are not supposed to mix? He's a spiritual giant and I'm just a pigmy. He's streets ahead of me. Wow! Fancy *him* asking me! And then I felt angry that he'd messed up my pursuit of the Holy Spirit. How could he do this? He had put me in a very awkward position. How could I say "no" graciously? And right at the end of all these thoughts was "How dare he?"

' "Excuse me, I have to go!" is what I said as I took off and ran!

'Back in my lodgings my mind was in turmoil. What *was* Paul thinking of? How could he be so mistaken? How could it be right for black and white to marry?

'I ran into the family prayer room. On the wall hung a big map of the world with pictures of all the missionaries my host family supported. Bang in the middle was a photo of a couple who were serving God in Jamaica – Mr and Mrs Michael Smith. He was white and she was black. I stared at it transfixed. So was it OK? Did God allow such a thing? It would seem that he did.

' "But Father, you told me not to marry."

' "No, I asked you if you were willing not to marry. There is a difference."

' "But I hardly know him. I don't love him."

'The response was immediate, "Yes you do."

'I sat astonished as my heavenly Father gave me an action replay of my first year in college. Paul was one of the first people I had met. He had been cleaning out the boilers and wore trousers that looked twice his size while his blazer looked two sizes too small. But he had a disarming smile and carried my luggage up to my room. I liked him. My mind flashed back to my "survey" of the male students. He was the only one I found appealing and the comment I had made to myself had been, "If Paul Jinadu were white, he would cause me some problems." But he wasn't, so he didn't! I blushed as I remembered what I had said.

'The Holy Spirit continued the conversation: "You admire him, don't you?"

' "More than any other person," came my reply.

' "You respect him?"

' "Totally."

' "You like him, admire him, respect him and enjoy his

company. Don't you know that these are the components of love?"

'Light was dawning. My mind went back four days when I had arrived to join the mission. I had no idea that Paul was part of the team, but it was he who was sent to meet me at the station. As he came striding towards me, my heart had leapt for joy. It had felt pretty close to love, but I discounted my feelings, rationalising that I was taken by surprise and it was a pleasure to work with someone I admired and trusted.

' "Lord, you've set me up!"

'These thoughts were all incredibly exciting and unexpected. My mind was still whirling, but there was one further problem.

' "Lord, if this is really you, I will need signs and wonders galore. I cannot afford to make a mistake. And, if this *is* you, Lord, it will be as if all hell has been let loose at home."

'The next day Paul asked, "May I have my answer?"

' "You will need to give me time. Please don't contact me for at least three months. I have so many issues to sort through and I really need to be certain that this is of God."

'I returned to college and Paul went off to Scotland to work with the Faith Mission. I told no one what I had been asked. I needed signs. I needed wonders. I needed *words from God*! I got them, and by November I knew that my destiny lay linked with Paul in marriage. We arranged to meet in the Christmas holiday and agreed that after our meeting we would approach my parents.

'I knew that there would be a massive explosion and there was. "You have gone too far. Go off and be a missionary if you must, but don't marry one of the natives."

' "What about the children?" my mother wailed. "You'll

be mixing the blood. They will be half-castes. The British will hate them and the Nigerians will hate them. They will have a terrible life."

'It was painful. I had to face the fact that I was bringing shame and embarrassment to the family. I wanted to react. I wanted to defend myself. I wanted to return accusation with counter-accusation. But only for a millisecond. The Holy Spirit stopped me: "Don't ever condemn your parents, remember your heart. If you judge your parents or anyone else, you are simply a hypocrite. Remember that you said you were the chief of sinners. You were riddled with pride and prejudice. You have been forgiven much. Don't now turn round and condemn them for the same thing I forgave in you. Freely you have received, freely give."

'I had a mental picture of myself standing on a chair. Hands on hips, looking down on my mother with scorn, judging her and finding her guilty.

' "You are right, dear Holy Spirit. I am in no position to condemn. I release and bless my parents. I release and bless all my detractors."

'It was wonderful. I felt gloriously and exuberantly free. I was embarking on a lifetime and lifestyle of forgiveness. I was entering, in a small way, into the Secret Place – into the "fellowship of Christ's sufferings". How often he had been unjustly accused, maligned and blasphemed, yet he had always responded with forgiveness, even paying the ultimate price on the cross: "Father, forgive them for they know not what they do." He never fought his corner: "Like a sheep that before its shearers is dumb, so he opened not his mouth" (Isa. 53:7, RSV). I now had some small understanding of what the Lord Jesus had faced. His family had called him mad. The religious leaders had despised him as an unlettered Galilean and had attributed his miraculous power to Satan. His dearest friends had betrayed him.

'Jesus understood everything that I was going through, but it didn't get to him and it need not get to me. I began to feel like a forgiveness philanthropist dispensing forgiveness to anyone I could find who needed it. I began to understand that forgiveness has rewards; that as I sow release and blessing, not only am I gloriously liberated from pain and distress, but also in blessing others, the blessing will return to me. They will be blessed; I will be blessed, and the devil is put to shame. Blessing opens the door for the Holy Spirit to work in the lives of those we forgive, and in forgiving I can expect and anticipate all kinds of rewards. As it happened, I was to discover that some of these blessings would not show up immediately. In fact, some took many years.

'It was now eighteen months since Paul had proposed and we were no further in reaching my parents' consent. My pastor, Doug Greenfield, was very supportive and, together with Paul, we held a series of meetings. My parents were adamant and, looking back, I can only sympathise with them. Not only were Paul and I from different races and backgrounds, but neither of us had any money. From my parents' perspective, here was a young man without money or qualifications who wanted to take their daughter to unimaginable deprivations in deepest Africa!

'It seemed fairly obvious that their consent would never come. So one day, feeling distraught and anxious, I sought sanctuary in one of York's many medieval churches. "Father," I prayed, "Let me just forget the whole thing. It is too difficult. It is causing too much pain. You asked me to be willing not to marry and I was fine with that. Let's just go back to that, shall we?"

' "If you do not have the courage to go through with this you may abandon it, but then you will be missing my perfect will for your life."

' "But Father, it is causing so much grief. So many people are against it, even some very prominent clergy."

' "You really love me, don't you?"

' "Yes."

' "You *only* want to please me?"

' "Yes."

' "Do you seriously suppose that I would allow you to go out of my will?"

'I looked up at one of the beautiful stained-glass windows. There was a text on it. It read: "Unto Him who is able to keep that which I have committed to Him".

' "You have entrusted your life to me. I am able to keep you and everything and everyone you commit to me."

'I was constantly amazed at the tender dealings of the Lord, and his continual love and reassurance was humbling.

' "Then make this marriage a glorious marriage and a blessing to all my family," I prayed.

'Some time later we informed my parents that the marriage would definitely take place. Sadly, we realised it had to go ahead without them; they still could not give their blessing.

'With just a week to go before our wedding, my distraught mother invited a very well-known clergyman to the house. He was there to talk to me and point out the error of my ways. He regarded me sorrowfully and told me I was making a huge mistake. When that failed, my mother took to her bed. She was close to a breakdown and informed me that if I went ahead, she would in all probability end up in a mental institution. I was asked to please leave the house.

' "I cannot countenance what you are doing," she said. "It

will drive me mad. I will end up in a mental home. You had better go."

'I was being thrown out! Never in a thousand years would I have imagined such a scenario. I was the firstborn, an adored and pampered child. Now I was the one to be in shock. My parents were against this marriage. At Bible College the staff were not enthusiastic and, as far as I knew, the prayer warrior was still keeping up her vigil. It all seemed very heavy.

'The Lord had provided Paul and me with a house. It was within walking distance of my parents' home. I made my way there with my few belongings, fell on my knees, and wept.

'Our wedding was just four days away. None of my family would be there, though my church family turned out in full force. I would not be able to walk down the aisle on my father's arm, so I decided I would walk down alone. My pastor had kindly offered to stand in, but I had told him that I didn't want anyone to take my father's place. "I'll come down alone with my bridesmaid," I had said.

'Alone in the silent house I wept my way through the psalms until I came to Psalm 27. I pictured the young David; the anointed king, yet on the run, pursued by Saul and 5,000 armed warriors. He was hiding in a cave surrounded by enemies. There was no way of escape.

'The words came rushing towards me like an express train:

> The Lord is my light and my salvation;
> whom shall I fear?
> The Lord is the strength of my life;
> of whom shall I be afraid?

Though an host should encamp against me,
my heart shall not fear:
though war should rise against me,
in this will I be confident.

One thing have I desired of the Lord,
that will I seek after;
that I may dwell in the house of the Lord all the days of
   my life,
to behold the beauty of the Lord,
and to inquire in his temple.

(Ps. 27:1, 3, 4, AV)

'Thirty-seven years later I find it hard to express the full impact of those words on my life. Verse 4 has become a loadstone, a guiding star to live by. I found a place of safety, peace and joy in the presence of the Lord Jesus Christ. He gave me the key to the "secret place" of his presence: a place of love, illumination, holiness and comfort.

'Song of Songs says, "He brought me into his banqueting house and his banner over me is love . . . I am my beloved's and he is mine." And so I found Jesus to be my first Lover, my first Husband, my Brother and my intimate Companion. I have been seeking to live in that secret place ever since. In verse 5 of that psalm, I read, "For in the time of trouble he shall hide me in his pavilion." A little further on: "In the secret place of his tabernacle shall he hide me." And then, "He shall set me upon a rock."

'I will never forget the love, acceptance and approval I felt coming from the Lord while all alone and on my knees with tears streaming down my face. The will of God is infinitely precious and his approval supersedes man's condemnation. I found a place where I could "snuggle into God" and let him take care of all my affairs.

'Over the next few hours I kept returning to read that psalm. Later, in verse 10, I read, "When my father and mother forsake me, the Lord will take me up."

'My heart was at peace, but I was still weeping. Weeping for my family, weeping for my detractors, and no doubt weeping for myself. My heart was peaceful, but I continued to weep.

'I carried on reading until I came to Psalm 45. I was in for another big surprise:

Listen, O daughter, and consider and incline your ear:
Forget your own people and your father's house:
So shall the King greatly desire your beauty.
He is your Lord. Worship him.

'Here I almost laughed aloud. No one, not even Paul, my future husband, had ever called me beautiful. But here was my Lord and Saviour declaring my beauty, affirming my value, and inviting me to become a life-long worshipper; his bride. He was showing me a whole new identity. My earthly parents were my caretakers, but my real genesis was in God the Father. I was "born again", not of blood, nor of the will of the flesh, but "of God".

'I was indeed a beautiful, longed-for, treasured child. He had chosen me before the foundation of the world to be a bride for his Son.

'I stopped crying and began to dance! It took some time for the wonder and enormity of these glorious truths to settle and to find a resting-place in my heart.

'But there was more! I read on:

Instead of your fathers will be your sons
Whom you shall make princes in all the earth.

'So no half-castes. We would produce princes – and so it has proved to be.

'When we forgive, we not only open up those opposing us to the anointing and favour of the Holy Spirit, but we open up ourselves to his outpouring. Out of our innermost being flow rivers of living water; rivers of blessing, rivers of healing, wholeness and intimacy with God. What I learned through persecution that morning long ago has been utterly life-transforming. Had pain not driven me "into God", I could have missed these blessings.

'Paul and I have now been married nearly thirty-eight years. When we returned from honeymoon my parents were waiting on our doorstep with words of love and reconciliation. Some time later they began attending the parish church and subsequently embraced the Lord Jesus as their personal Lord and Saviour. Our two children are indeed "princes". It's a bit of a family joke, but anyone who knows them will admit that right from birth God's favour has been evident in their lives. My mother, at ninety-four, is a proud mum, a much-loved grandma and a great grandmama.

'Some time before she died, my loquacious aunt came to London on a visit and I took her to the Tower Thistle Hotel for lunch. She asked if she could bring a friend. The friend and I ate while Auntie talked. I listened with fascination as my aunt rehearsed the achievements of the Jinadu family. Our work in Nigeria, and church planting in three continents, was examined in detail. Then she went on to our sons. Incredulously I heard her recite their O-levels, A-levels and university degrees. Things I had long forgotten were brought out and wondered at. I found it very amusing as I remembered all her dire prognostications before the wedding. "She's forgotten everything she said," I concluded.

'In our thirty-eight years together as husband and wife, Paul and I have had plenty of opportunity to exercise forgiveness and have come to the conclusion that indeed all things are forgivable. In the early years of marriage we experienced heartache; and in the ministry we have experienced pain, betrayal and false accusations. As God-fearers, we dare not withhold forgiveness. Time and time again we have proved that "all things work together for good to those who love God who are called according to his purposes", and that releasing and forgiving one's accusers always brings a blessing. After all, "love never fails".

'I have learnt that forgiveness is a lifestyle that has *great* rewards.'

3

Praying with the Enemy
– Sister Claire-Edith de la Croix

Today, Sister Claire-Edith de la Croix is a nun in the Monastery of Saint Clare in Jerusalem. But in that, she is unusual because she is Jewish. In fact, she is from an American Orthodox Jewish family. Her life has been punctuated by tragedy after painful tragedy. I didn't realise this when I first met her at the monastery, almost by accident. I was there to interview another sister for another book! That sister spoke French and Sister Claire-Edith, being a fluent French speaker, offered to translate. She wasn't actually a 'proper' nun then. She was awaiting formal entrance into the monastic community. I suppose she was really making sure she was ready to take the final step of leaving all that is worldly behind before entering fully into a life of prayer and solitude.

We corresponded for a while and when I told Sister Claire-Edith that I was compiling a book of stories of forgiveness with R.T. Kendall, she volunteered her story. I had no idea then what her story entailed – I could never have imagined. Not only has she had to forgive others for the harm done to her, she has also had to forgive herself.

So, while in Jerusalem on a recent trip, I went along to the monastery, which is situated in the Talpiot region of Jerusalem on the road to Bethlehem. I entered through the imposing gate in the wall into the quiet and deeply spiritual world of the sisters who live there. The path up to the front door is fringed by overhanging trees and plants. Overgrown and unkempt in a pleasant way, there's a calmness about the place which contrasts with the frenetic pace of life outside.

I was shown into the room where Sister Claire-Edith would come and meet me. I hadn't seen her in her habit before. The last time we met she had been in civvies and called by her 'previous' name – the name her parents had given her; Sister Claire-Edith de la Croix is the name she chose to adopt when she became a nun. I wondered what she would look like.

On entering the room, I was immediately taken aback. There was a metal grill across the middle of the room. Seconds later, Sister Claire-Edith entered the room from the other side. She opened the grill to shake my hand. 'Why do we have to be separated like this?' I asked.

'It's normal,' she smiled. I could tell she was content and left it at that. Having volunteered to tell me her story, she seemed keen to get on with it. Nothing could have prepared me for what I was about to hear:

'I was born in the mid-1950s in the United States into an ultra-Orthodox Jewish family and I lived as a strictly practising and believing Orthodox Jew. It's important to understand what it was like being brought up in such a religiously devout family because today when people use the word "religious" it's as though they're meaning the opposite of "believing". But that's not what I mean when I use the word "religious" in this context. My family had a very strong belief in God and this was demonstrated in their religious observance. At home we strictly – and lovingly – observed Shabbat, Kashrut, and all the other religious laws. Saying the Blessings defines the day for an Orthodox Jew. For instance, when you take any nourishment, even a sip of water, there's a blessing before and a blessing after. Even when you go to the bathroom there's a beautiful blessing. It's wonderful: "Blessed are you, O Lord our God, King of the universe. Who created mankind in wisdom. Who created us with vesicles and valves so that if any of them are unduly open or any of them are unduly closed we would not be able to exist and be able to stand before you and your throne of grace. Blessed are you, Lord our God, who does wonders." Isn't that great? It's a wonderful blessing, and you say that several times a day obviously.

'So I grew up in this Orthodox background. My mother had an ongoing conversation with God out loud and it never occurred to me that she was actually "praying"; to me she was just talking to God because he was in the room with her – it seemed so natural and so real. She called him Ribono shel Olam – Master of the universe, Sovereign of the universe. She would be ironing my father's shirts, and my father was very particular about his collars, so as she was ironing she would say, "O Master of the universe, I'm ironing my husband's shirts and you know how he gets, so please help me with that!" When my brother and I went off to school she would say, "My children are going to school now, O Master of the universe, and you know Victory Boulevard is very busy at this time of the day, so please make sure nobody hits them and make sure the crossing guard is paying attention." God's presence was very real to her.

'My father was an undercover government agent

investigating illegal international arms dealing. I realise now that I grew up in a non-standard family, although at the time it never occurred to me that anything was unusual.

When I was fourteen it was decided that I was wasting my time in secondary school, and so they arranged for me to sit the entrance exams to go to university. And so it was that a month before I was fifteen I started university.'

'You were exceptional in other words?' I asked.

'Unusual.'

'Were you pushed or was it natural?'

'Oh no, it was as natural as breathing. Today, looking back, I don't think it was a good idea because I was emotionally and socially so far behind my fellow students. It would have been much better to keep me in secondary school and let me take enrichment classes or private lessons or private study projects or something. I don't recommend it, I don't think it's a good idea.'

'Did you feel isolated?'

'Well, I was an Orthodox Jew, a little girl at an American University in 1970 – we're talking sex, drugs, demonstrations, Vietnam – I was way out of my element!

'I became active in the anti-war movement. I started writing leaflets and marching in the streets and got arrested once during a demonstration. They were arresting us by the hundreds and sticking us in a parking lot. They arrested us and sent us through one entrance, but we ran away through another entrance, so maybe *detained* is the right word.

'After I completed my first degree, I continued advanced studies, even after my marriage at the age of nineteen.

'My husband and I were so happy. He was twenty-one, a social worker and a teacher. We had three children. In 1983 we went to a Purim feast and, as was the custom, my husband drank, so he asked me to drive home. There was a terrible accident and my husband and children died. I was hurt, but not very badly; I was thrown free from the car. My children were eight, six and four years old; two older boys and then my little girl.

'I lost my mind for a short time. I became very depressed and very angry, but this is where the belief comes in that I was talking about earlier, because I never lost my faith in God. No merit to me, it's God who does that. It's grace; it's a gift. It comes from him. I screamed at God. I ranted. I raved. I swore at him, I cursed him. I used all the horrible language I had picked up at university – but nevertheless God was just as present to me as he was to my mother. He was there. You can't be angry with someone who doesn't exist, and you can't rage at someone with whom you don't have a relationship. It was a hard school. But God is there – he stays there. He is constant, and he is so much bigger than we are and he can handle it, all our rage.

'I was twenty-eight. The accident happened on the annual Jewish feast of Purim which fell in March and, in June, I came to live in Israel. There's a saying in the Talmud, "Change of place, change of fortune". I just wanted out. I left everything behind in the United States. I didn't bring photos, I didn't bring anything. I asked my family to sell the house and I used what I had from the sale to pay off the debts. Looking back, I wish I had saved something. A picture. Something. I've got no tangible memory of that time, yet I see through all of this the golden thread of God in my life.

'I still have times of feeling terribly guilty. Forgiving myself is an ongoing process. There was no one else involved in the accident. I lost control of the car and we left the road. I had no one to blame but myself. And God. I blamed him a lot.

Why me, why did this happen to me? Why did you do this to me, God?

'And so I came to Israel on a one-way ticket with one hundred dollars. An impulsive thing to do, but why not? I thought to myself: "I'm Jewish, they have to take me." First of all I went to a kibbutz to learn modern Hebrew; I knew biblical Hebrew, but people stared at me when I spoke. Imagine somebody going around speaking Chaucerian English! They didn't exactly point and laugh, but close!

'By now it was 1983 and the kibbutz I lived on was Ramat Rachel, near here, on the south side of Jerusalem overlooking Bethlehem. And then I went to another kibbutz, Kibbutz Shamir in the north, for a short time and then I went to live in Nazareth Ilit. Then I came back to Jerusalem. I took all sorts of menial jobs. I worked at a falafel stand scrubbing pots, washing floors, and making coffee for the Arab who was in charge of the kitchen. Then I worked on an assembly line in the Elite Candy factory. This was actually great fun. It was so neat – these waffle cookies came off the assembly line in little packets. We were four women and each of us had a stack of unfolded boxes. So we had to take a box off the stack, fold it, take the package and put it in, close the box, and put it away. It was timed so that each of these four steps was being carried out by these four women in sequence. It was like a dance that had been carefully choreographed. It was so precise – a small role, yet all about being part of something bigger; like marching in formation, being in a drill team, or dancing with a group, or playing in an orchestra.

'As for the other women, one was Romanian and the other two were Arabs. We didn't have any language in common so we sort of got by in versions of Hebrew. I stuck it out, because I enjoyed the actual work. I know it sounds funny but it was very relaxing, very meditative and very graceful. But the way the bosses treated us was dreadful. I lived directly across the road from the factory – you could stand at the gate and look in the window of my living room. But I was not allowed to leave the premises for lunch. They locked the gate at the beginning of the shift and they unlocked it at the end of the shift. If you needed to use the bathroom, you had to raise your hand and get permission. I couldn't take all that regimentation, so after a few months I quit. I walked out one morning in disgust. It's very funny that I am in a monastery because I have a long history of rebelling against structure!

'Anyway, I left the factory and got a job as a Hebrew-English secretary and then as a translator. It was around this time, 1988, that I was on a bus from Haifa to Jerusalem, along the coastal road, and unbeknown to all on board, a bomb had been planted on the bus. The bomb was underneath the bus, under the driver's seat. I was sitting two seats behind the driver. Miraculously no one was killed; even the driver was not seriously wounded. I heard the noise. I looked at the driver. His seat was gone so he was standing up. The back of his previously white shirt was covered in blood. I was thrown up by the force of the explosion and landed bent backwards over a seat with a whole lot of people on top of me.

'At first I thought I was dead. Then I thought the guy on top of me was dead. Then he moved and I realised that neither one of us was dead. And then I thought I was about to die, so I started saying the Hebrew form of confession that we say on Yom Kippur, as much as I could remember of it. And I started saying the Shema Israel. I heard other people praying and a woman screaming. And then I heard her husband telling her to shut up; I was aware of all kinds of reactions. Gradually people got off me and I stood up. I didn't realise then that I was wounded. I was once a trained nurse and there were wounded people around me; instinctively I started to give help. There was one man who was very badly wounded. His leg was almost severed. I only realised that I myself was badly injured when I got back to Jerusalem, and for the next seven years I depended on painkillers to numb the constant agony. I had an operation on my spine but, even so, I spent much of my time in a wheelchair, and when I did manage to stand up, I kept falling; I couldn't stand for very long, my legs just wouldn't hold me.

'Shortly after this, and while still struggling with the pain in my back, I married a Hasidic rabbi; an ultra-Orthodox Jew like myself. A physicist, he was originally a university lecturer, but when he came to live in Israel he was ordained a rabbi, although he still taught physics on the side. He was a year or so younger than me. We were introduced by another rabbi who took it upon himself to find me a husband from among the single guys he knew with PhDs. He figured it wasn't good for a wife to have more education than her husband! My husband wasn't the first man that this rabbi had suggested; I had already turned down several. But I thought I would meet the physicist, and my first impressions were positive. He was so cute! I remember he did a Charlie Chaplin impression in the middle of the street once while we were waiting for a bus. And I thought, yes, he's my kind of guy.

'However, it's not the same as when you're nineteen. A nineteen-year-old virgin, as he was, and a thirty-two-year-old widow, as I was, do not have a lot in common. But our early married life was good, it was pleasant, it was respectful, we were friendly and we liked each other – until I became a believer.

'By that time we were heavily involved with what's called

the Kiruv Movement; Kiruv means "bringing closer". This involved introducing non-observant, non-practising, assimilated young Jews to God and to Jewish observance. The main way we did that was by feeding them – in all senses of the word, but particularly in the physical sense. Mostly they were students travelling through Israel because they wanted to get away from home and their parents had paid for a ticket to Israel rather than to South America or India. Some were New Age, others were hippies. We would offer them a free meal and they would come. My husband was a vegetarian and I was not, so I could accommodate any bizarre diet. I made vegetarian food in traditional Jewish style, making knishes out of soya instead of meat for example. It was a good experience.

'We would have about fifteen guests for every meal on Shabbat – three meals. The particular stream of Orthodox Judaism we followed did not allow the washing of dishes on Shabbat, which meant every Saturday evening there were a lot of dirty dishes to clear up. My own particular way of doing things was to have everything clean and tidy by the time my husband came home from the synagogue so that we could welcome the week together in a nice environment.

'So I was washing dishes one Saturday night and had a desire to hear English. I turned on the radio and I tuned in to the BBC World Service. It so happened that this was during Lent, although I had no idea about such things at that time. Just before the programme I wanted to hear was "Words of Faith". Now the content of "Words of Faith" did not usually contain strong gospel preaching, but on this particular occasion there was somebody talking about Jesus on the cross and he said that at Calvary Jesus offered himself as the ultimate sin offering.

'That spoke to me, and all of a sudden I was there; I was up to my elbows in soapy water, literally paralysed. Everything I had ever learned from the Talmud, from the Bible, which to me of course was the Old Testament, from the writings of the Jewish sages, the rabbinical writings, all of a sudden made sense. There is a Talmudic principle that God always provides the cure before the illness; the remedy before the plague. I thought, wait a minute, Jesus was crucified just before the temple was destroyed. After the temple was destroyed we couldn't have the order of sacrifice any more. But God had already provided the remedy; we didn't need the order of sacrifice any longer – that was Jesus.

'All my life, I hope I have made it clear, I only wanted to be with God. Even when I was angry at God, he was still right there. So, in that moment I realised I had made a mistake. My spiritual eyes were suddenly opened and I understood that all the effort involved in minute ritual observance was not what God wanted. God wants obedience, not sacrifice. I needed to find out about this. I consider that at that moment I became a Christian – a believer.

'Prior to this I had been an anti-missionary activist here in Jerusalem so I knew there was a group calling themselves Messianic Jews and I knew that on a particular street in Jerusalem there was a building where they met. Therefore I decided to look for them in the phone book. I didn't know exactly what they were called; I knew the name of the street and I knew they had the word "Messianic" in their name. So I took the Hebrew phone book and I started at Aleph and I read every name on every page, looking for something that had the name "Messianic" in it on this particular street. It took a few days because I eventually found it near the end, under "Kof", which is the fourth to last letter of the Hebrew alphabet. By doing this, I also gained an intimate knowledge of who lives in Jerusalem! I called the number and here another miracle happened. A woman answered and I said, "I just want to find out . . . I don't want to become a Christian. I don't want to convert. I am a Jew. I want to stay a Jew, but I want to find out. Can I meet you?" I later found out that the number I called was in a room where usually no one was present. It was unheard of for this woman, who was the wife of one of the elders of the congregation, to be there . . . it was one of God's things with a capital T. So I met with her and we read the Gospel of John together.

'I had read this Gospel before during my university studies, but then my interest was merely academic. This time the gospel message resounded in my heart, confirming my new belief. A year later, I was baptised.

'During that first year, once I understood that Jesus was the Messiah and that he's God, I had to tell my husband because I wanted him to know about this revelation too. However, this turned out to be not a good idea because he began to beat me. You have to remember that I was still injured as a result of the bus bombing, spending a lot of time in a wheelchair and still taking large quantities of painkillers. Also, we had a cat and he would put my New Testament in the cat's litter box. As well as beating me, he began to perform Kabalistic rites against me; Kabalism is a particularly dark side of Judaism. I was being attacked physically and spiritually. There's a very dark side to Kabala. Shortly after I was baptised I was asleep and dreamt that my husband was standing over me and stabbing me with a big knife. I opened my eyes and there he was standing by me with a book of Kabalistic incantations, reading these things over me. I felt that was really dangerous. I said to him, "I am covered in the blood of Jesus and you can't do anything to me, take that into the other room." I had never before spoken to him in that commanding tone, but he silently obeyed and left the room. A couple of days after that I ran away. I knew it was no longer safe for me to stay with him, and the elders of my congregation agreed.

'For several months I moved around, staying in believers' homes and looking for work. I did experience some persecution from the anti-missionary group that I had previously worked with. For instance, I found a job as a translator for the Ministry of Tourism and members of this group began making security complaints against me in order to get me sacked.

'Gradually, despite the pain in my back, I re-established myself in the workplace and eventually ended up running my own translation business.

Also, I became a Catholic.

'Once I was invited to a prayer meeting and told that they were Catholics. "They are charismatic, they pray in tongues," I was told, although I didn't know what that meant, "and they are French." So I went along and, to me, it was an entirely new experience and it was very interesting. But when they first sang in tongues, I thought they were singing in French!

'I began to visit them regularly. They did not make any attempt to influence my belief; rather, they only talked about what they believed . . . but only if I insisted. I need to say, and this is really important, that Jesus said there are many rooms in my Father's house, and I think we have to take that seriously; I think we are all in the Father's house. For me, it was important to have continuity with the Church that Jesus started, and for me, with my needs and in my context, I found that continuity in the Catholic Church. I do not rule out anyone else, and even Catholic teaching of today no longer says that salvation is only found in the Catholic Church.

'At the same time as I decided to become a Catholic, I was still being persecuted by the anti-missionary people and chased from one job to another and from one apartment to another. On one occasion I was physically attacked – it was a horrible time. Also, I was still in severe pain as a result of the spinal injury caused by the bus bombing in 1988.

'So, in order to feel safe, I decided to go and live with this community for a few months while preparing to enter the Catholic Church. In the community I was the only Jew, but it was a community that had a great love for Israel. They organised a Shabbat service every Friday evening with candles, wine and bread, and also the ceremony that closes Shabbat every Saturday evening, saying all the prayers in Hebrew. One of the people in the community was a person I am calling Pauline. Pauline was born in a Palestinian Authority area; a brilliant young woman, she hadn't received the education she deserved. She couldn't get permission to come and live in Israel permanently, and her family didn't really want her to in any case. She resented the Israeli occupation. She was deeply attached to the land, the Holy Land, and her family was nominally Christian. As a teenager she was recruited by a Palestinian group of fighters during the first intifada and, being very gifted, she quickly rose to being a person of authority in charge of other adolescents who were sent out on raids to throw Molotov cocktails at passing Israeli buses. From what I understand, she believed the land of Palestine was identified with God and the Palestinians were the chosen people. She was fighting for the land, for her people and her God against the bad Jews, the demonic Jews.

'Eventually, Pauline was arrested by the Israeli army and sent to prison and held as a security prisoner, which is no joke. She described how she was pushed around and humiliated; for a proud, bright girl and a modest young woman, it was a horrible experience. She served her time, she was released, and she went back home to her family. There she met someone who read the Bible, and she too started reading the Bible and eventually became a committed Christian.

'She came to East Jerusalem and somehow met members of this same community which was then situated on the border between East Jerusalem and West Jerusalem. She ended up joining, and was already there when I arrived. She saw me and I saw her and we sort of looked at each other and shook hands. We avoided contact as much as was reasonably possible, which had a dreadful effect on our spiritual lives and on our prayer lives because we were not in the light. We slept in rooms next to each other, ate together at the table, prayed together, worshipped together and despised each other while pretending not to, which is even worse because it added hypocrisy to hate. We avoided outright conflict, but also any sort of contact because we assumed that contact would result in conflict.

'At this time I was still quite handicapped and walking with a walker and there was a hill behind the house where we lived. I really wanted to climb that hill. I do not remember how it happened, but Pauline ended up helping me up this hill. Since we were living together in the community, she knew my story and I knew hers. We started talking. She said something about my injury and I said something like, "Well, you know, it wasn't an accident – someone put a bomb on the bus that I was riding in and it was a Palestinian that did that." We went through a period of mutual accusations. "Why do your people want to take the land away from my people?" We could each say that. We got really angry. You have already gathered that I am not a meek sort of person and neither was she! We both knew how to use words to hurt and we used them, as weapons. But then the Holy Spirit wouldn't allow that to happen for much longer and we suddenly stopped and both started crying, and through the tears we began talking. We moved beyond the anger to the next level of pain, fear, mistrust and insecurity. Then we hugged; we held each other as we were crying – it was as though we were suspended in a moment of time, just the two of us sharing our mutual feelings of pain and loss.

'I can't remember exactly how it happened, but we both thought of the verse in Ephesians 2 (verse 14) that describes Jesus as our peace – "For he himself is our peace, who has made the two one and has destroyed the barrier, the dividing wall of hostility . . . His purpose was to create in himself one new man out of the two, thus making peace, and in this one body to reconcile both of them to God through the cross by which he put to death their hostility."

'He made the two into one. Well, what were we to do with that? It seemed to us that we don't actually do anything with it. It's Jesus who did it. It's God who did it. It's not us. All we can do is stand there in front of it.

'We also thought of the verse in Zechariah (12:10) – "I will pour out on the house of David and the inhabitants of Jerusalem a spirit of grace and supplication. They will look on me, the one they have pierced, and they will mourn for him as one mourns for an only child, and grieve bitterly for him as one grieves for a firstborn son."

'So those verses came to both of us at the same time. It was just one of those things where the Holy Spirit was really working hard to get us past our nonsense. It struck us both as funny and we started giggling and later we went into the chapel arm in arm to pray together, and we since have become friends – not close friends, but friends.

'Soon after that experience, one evening I listened as the person who was in charge of the community talked about the time Jesus fed the crowd of 4,000 (Mark 8) and how on this occasion it was Jesus who noticed that the people were hungry. The initiative was his. Rather than waiting for his disciples to bring the need to his attention, Jesus acted out of his own desire to give us everything we need. The speaker was explaining that Jesus wants to give us gifts and we simply have to accept them. I saw very clearly that God was speaking through her to me. Precisely to me. And so I started praying: "OK, Jesus, I guess you want to give me something." Now at that time I thought what he wanted to give me was suffering in order to purify me. So I said, "Whatever you want from me I am willing to accept it. I want it. If it comes from you, I want it."

'I started praying then, and I continued praying for the rest of the evening. I went to bed praying, and the next morning I was healed. I woke up and, without thinking, I got up and walked over to the window without my sticks, without the heavy metal back brace . . . and without any pain. At first I thought I must have damaged my back in the night without realising it and damaged the nerves. I thought I was going to fall. Then I felt a hand supporting my back and preventing me from falling. And that was that. I was healed. The pain had disappeared!

'It happened soon after I'd forgiven Pauline, on the night I learnt to be willing to receive the gifts that Jesus wants to give us.

'It's important for me to say that the main part of the healing was not the physical healing – that was like the icing on the cake. Rather, it was the seal on a profound inner healing. It utterly changed my relationship with God; it was the difference between being engaged and being married. I had been very depressed and angry, and now I wasn't depressed or angry any longer. The physical healing was almost incidental. I also had a milk allergy that went away, and my eyesight improved! But the most profound thing was the inner healing. The outer healing just expressed that.

'For the first time in my life I was free from unforgiveness, whether of myself, my second husband, or Pauline. The effects were startling.

'For several years I carried on my translation business before visiting the Monastery of Saint Clare for the first time, but I didn't stay. Then in 2002, on Palm Sunday, I entered here definitively. God willing, in spring 2005, I will take vows of poverty, chastity, obedience and enclosure.

'And why am I here? I believe I am standing in the gap in the sense that we read about in the book of Jeremiah; constantly bringing the world before the throne of grace, and then reminding the world that God is there and he is in control. As contemplative nuns, we are called to be a conduit for two-way communication and a prophetic sign. When I talk to Israelis who are not even religious they accept that, they understand that there's a need for that. I am also here to pray for Jewish Israelis and Arab Israelis and for Arab Palestinians; I am praying for the two peoples. I offer the experiences and sacrifices of my life for the two peoples and for their reconciliation under the sovereign God. I am not engaged as some are in dialogue with a capital "D". My call is different. My call is to intercessory prayer. That was my call before I became a Catholic and God doesn't change his mind.'

4

A Life Transformed
– Maron Raheb

Maron was once a drug addict living in the Old City of Jerusalem where a sense of hopelessness, coupled with a seething hatred of Jews, pervaded every thought and persuaded every action of his life. If life had taken its natural course of events, Maron would be dead. He had no will to live; no expectations in life. But something happened to change his life for ever.

He invited me to visit him and his family in their home on the outskirts of Jerusalem. His German wife is called Angelika, and they have two beautiful, vivacious children. They live in a smart apartment. They have no regular income, but they are short of nothing. When I asked Maron how they manage, he told me God is faithful and he provides. Maron is an evangelist today, spending much of his time in nearby Jericho, sharing his story with the Muslims who live there.

He is a quiet, thoughtful man. Still relatively young, life has taken him along an often dangerous path. He sat quietly and closed his eyes while Angelika passed around cups of tea. Then, settled into his armchair, we sat and talked, as he fought with the exhaustion that wanted to creep over him. He told me it was the first time he'd stopped in days. His wife agreed. She doesn't see much of him as he works long hours, frequently travelling in and out of Jericho, which is now in the West Bank under Palestinian authority control. But today this former drug addict, who at one time couldn't have cared whether he lived or died, is driven on by a sense of urgency to reach his own Arab people with the gospel message of peace and reconciliation. And perhaps most amazing of all, he bears no animosity towards the Jews . . . in fact, he works closely with a number of Jewish believers. More than that, he makes it a priority to do so because he believes this is what God has called him to do. So how has he overcome his hatred and bitterness; how has he managed to not only forgive, but come to love a people who in the normal course of events, he has every reason to despise?

Here is Maron's story . . . told in his own words:

'My name is Maron Raheb and I am from the Old City of Jerusalem. My wife is called Angelika, she's from Germany, and we live north of Jerusalem on the road to Ramallah.

'I am serving the Lord as an evangelist in many places; in Jerusalem, in Jericho and in Ramleh, near Tel Aviv, where I lead a home group for twenty-five people who come every Saturday night to hear the word of the Lord. This group has grown very quickly and many people are now wanting to come, so we are searching for a bigger house!

'I am working with Campus Crusade and also with the Alliance Church in Jerusalem. In fact, what I do is I go into a new situation and start something, then other people come along behind me and take over. I suppose I'm a ground breaker!

'How I came to be working as a Christian evangelist is

quite a story. I am a Palestinian, born in Jerusalem. My family were originally from Ramleh. Then in 1948, during the war here, they escaped from Ramleh and went to live in the Old City of Jerusalem. My parents used to own land in Ramleh, so after the fighting had stopped and things were a little calmer, my parents returned to see their land only to find it had been confiscated by the Israeli government. My mother went to the Israeli authorities to ask for this land to be returned to the family, but she was informed that they could not give her the land as it now belonged to Israel. She was told that if she wanted the land again she would have to buy it. But my parents didn't have that sort of money and so she left and came back to Jerusalem to start a new life; it was a difficult time.

'We were a nominal Christian family. I had seven sisters and two brothers and we all lived together in one room that measured three square metres. We had no electricity and there was often friction. And many times I had nowhere to sleep, so I slept outside in the street. And so it was that I grew up as a refugee.

'We were very poor at that time and my father didn't have a profession. He searched for work to try and earn a little money, but the doors were usually closed in his face; life just after the war was very difficult. But eventually he found work as a cook in a hotel. Then he got a job with some Israelis, working as a security guard, and they gave him a gun. They gave him a *gun* – he was an *Arab*, and they gave him a gun!

'When I was growing up and still living with my family in the Old City, there was a growing, menacing problem – drugs. Many people were using drugs, including my brother, Abraham. He became a drug addict and started to do things that did not please my family, and eventually my father threw him out of the house.

'Abraham ended up in prison, but something extraordinary happened to him there. My eldest sister visited him and gave him a Bible. Soon after, we heard he had given his life to Jesus Christ, and when he left prison he started to be an evangelist. He went from place to place talking about the Lord! It amazed me.

'Watching what happened to my brother had a big impact on my life because I too had begun to take soft drugs occasionally; in the Old City they were so easy to get hold of, everybody was taking them. And many people were dying too; people that I knew.

'As a teenager, I was always fighting with my father. I had a bitterness in my heart towards him – I didn't like him. He was a tough man. He often beat me and would throw me out of the house. Sometimes in the winter I had nowhere to sleep. I couldn't go home. I was cold. Then one day, when I was looking for somewhere to sleep, I met somebody who I'd known at school. He told me he was sleeping in a hotel and he invited me to join him. I was so grateful to him for offering me accommodation that I jumped at the opportunity. However, I soon realised that he was taking hard drugs. I watched as he injected himself, and soon after I started to use the drugs with him. I was twenty-three years old.

'Looking back, I can only say I felt in such a hopeless situation. My father used to tell me I was no good; even as a young child I was told I was no good. It seemed as though he was always shouting at me, saying I would never succeed in life. In fact, when I was small, they put me in an orphanage – they gave me away. But I escaped. It was a difficult life then; there was nothing to give me hope or encouragement. I had no expectations for my own life and I had such hatred in my heart towards my father; I didn't like him and he didn't like me.

'I'm sometimes asked if I hated my father more than the Jews when I was growing up. After all, I was told time and time again that it was the Jews who had robbed my family of their land and caused us so much hardship. I remember being with my friend, when we were teenagers, and we would often speak about the Jews and what they did to our families, how they destroyed many things and how they made our lives miserable. We always spoke negatively about the Israelis and many times I tried to write things against them on the walls of buildings. Sometimes we would go out on to the streets to throw stones at them and do bad things to them. One day I was walking along the street and a group of Israeli soldiers noticed me. Now on this occasion I wasn't doing anything; I was simply returning from my job. But one of the soldiers took hold of me and started to hit me and to beat me and I didn't know why. Other soldiers came to join him and they all started to beat me and they broke my face with their beatings. After that experience, the hatred that was already inside me started to increase and increase and I vowed I would never love those people because they were my enemy; they did wrong things to me; it was too difficult for me to love them.

'Things went from bad to worse. I hated my father. I hated Jews. I was a heroin addict; I drank a lot of alcohol; I took any drug I could get my hands on. I used to steal and did a lot of bad things to get the money I needed to buy drugs. I was very skinny, and looked close to death; I later heard that my mother was told, by people who knew me, to prepare for my burial. I had reached the lowest point in my life.

'I was arrested and sent to prison – many times. But each time I was released after only a few days and went straight back to taking drugs . . . more and more and more.

'Looking back on my life now, I think one of the biggest problems faced by Arabs is that they believe they are not loved. Here in Israel, so many Christians come who have a love for the Jews, and Arabs are left with the impression that there's nobody who is really interested in us Arabs. So we ask the question, "Does God have favourites?" I can remember watching television reports about trouble in Gaza or the West Bank and wondering why God was allowing the Palestinian people to suffer so much. It made me so angry.

'My view on life started to shift when my father became a Christian and I saw a huge change in him, which surprised me. He died shortly afterwards, sadly before he saw a change in me. But seeing him mellow and become so sweet-natured really shocked me and I started to wonder about my own life. Could I change too? Could I make something of my life? Could I ever kick the drug habit and be somebody, and do something worthwhile?

'And so it was that shortly after my father died, I agreed, reluctantly, to visit a rehabilitation centre (House of Victory) in Haifa run by believers, and it was there that I met the Lord, and there that the Lord changed my life. It didn't happen all at once; when I arrived and looked around I thought I would stay for one week and then escape! But you know, the Lord did things with me, wonderful things.

'One day, I was lying on my bed and I had a dream. I felt something over my body that was trying to stifle me. In my dream I called to one of the guys to help me. He called David Davies (Director of the House of Victory), but he was doing something else and couldn't come to me. I was starting to panic because I felt this "thing" was smothering me, so I called to Jesus for help and immediately this "thing" left me. When I woke up I realised I'd had a nightmare, but Jesus had come to me and rescued me and that experience persuaded me that perhaps I should stay in the House of Victory and finish the rehab programme.

'I was in for many more surprises. Shortly after this, it was time for the week-long Biblical Feast of Tabernacles when traditionally Jewish families build a shelter, or booth, in their garden where they have all their meals. It's a sort of harvest festival, when the Jewish people remember the goodness of God and give thanks for the ingathering of the harvest. One of the guys at the rehab centre, Danny, who was Jewish, asked me to help him build one of these shelters in the garden. Without a moment's hesitation I happily agreed. As I was helping him, I realised I was finding it a pleasure. It occurred to me that previously, before I had become a Christian, I would have wanted to destroy this Jewish guy – now I loved him like my own brother. I asked myself how this could be . . . and I realised that since I had given my life to Jesus Christ, he was living in me and changing my attitudes in a radical way.

'After I finished my rehab programme in Haifa, I won a scholarship to study the Bible at a college run by the Assemblies of God. I came back to Jerusalem and began my studies at the same time as working alongside other pastors connected to the Alliance Church there. Two years later I met Angelika, and before long we were married and I started working full time as an evangelist. But I found I still had a problem. My wife is German and together we attended many conferences both here in Israel and in other countries. On one occasion we went to Germany, and I quickly discovered that many German Christians love Israel and the Jewish people. So wherever we went, there was the Israeli flag fluttering in front of our faces. As soon as I saw this flag I would feel myself reacting; I would close up because I felt it was just another Christian Zionist conference. Why did they have the Israeli flag there; why didn't they have the Palestinian flag? I would think to myself that it wasn't a conference for Jews, it was a conference for European Christians, so why did they have the Israeli flag? As an Arab Christian, I found this so offensive that I would not be able to concentrate on what was being said during the conference.

'After that particular conference in Germany, I remember coming back to Jerusalem with all this resentment and hatred in my heart. I was sharing how I felt with an Arab Christian friend and he said to me, "Maron, you know you cannot keep asking why, why, why, because you're really questioning God. God chose the Jewish people to live in this country. You must not hate them; you cannot reject the will of God. You must love them too." As my friend shared his testimony with me I asked the Lord to take this bitterness from me and to help me love them.

'Shortly after this, I was driving with my wife in the car when an Israeli soldier stopped me and asked to see my identity card. His behaviour was quite aggressive towards me. He walked around the car, so I got out to talk to him. After checking my car and my ID, he eventually said to me, "If your daughter and your wife were not with you, I would kill you." In that moment I felt a resurgence of all the anger and bitterness I had once felt towards Jews threatening me once again. I wondered why he was saying these things. But then I heard the voice of the Lord telling me to stop, and instead he was urging me to pray for this guy and bless him and love him, and I found myself saying, "Lord, I love this guy and I pray for this guy," and immediately the Lord started to heal many things in my heart.

'But that wasn't the end of it! I only had to watch the news on the television to realise I had bitterness in my heart against Prime Minister Sharon and his government. One day I voiced my displeasure about government policy towards the Palestinians with some Arab Christian friends and they reminded me that God chose Sharon to be the leader of the Israeli government; God had put him in this position and it wasn't for me to reject the will of God. If he had put him in this position, then it was my duty to bless him and to love him. So I said, "Lord, how can I do that? But if it's your will, I will do it."

'Later that evening when I got home, I switched on the television to watch the news. The first picture I saw was of Prime Minister Sharon, and I remember I put out my hand and prayed for him, that the Lord would bless him and be with him, protect him and give him the wisdom he needed to lead his nation. I was pleased that I was able to pray like that because I knew it was the work of the Lord, the work of the Holy Spirit in my heart. I couldn't have said those words in my power, by my wisdom, by my strength. I cannot love him, I cannot forgive him, but through the Holy Spirit, through God, through Jesus Christ himself, I can love him, I can forgive him and I can pray for him.

'Today I can say that I genuinely love my Jewish brothers and sisters, not only the believers, but also those who are living here in this country. My job now is to pray for these people and to bless these people.

'I believe God wants the Arab and Jewish believers to come together in a display of unity. It doesn't please him to see us divided by hostility. God wants us to come together under his umbrella and for us to praise him together in unity and to love one another.

'It's important that we don't become political people. If we continually get side-tracked by the pressure of politics, then these other things get lost. But if we focus on the Lord and if we really have the intention of reflecting Jesus and his will, then this will happen; this is what really unites.

'I believe God wants to teach us Arabs and Jews how to forgive each other and live in unity because we are living in the last days and Jesus will be returning soon. I remember the prayer that Jesus Christ prayed in John 17: "Let them be one as you and I are one." That's what Jesus Christ wants. He wants us all to be one in his body. It doesn't matter what kind of nation or what kind of tongue, but he wants to bring us together and for us to love one another and to have fellowship together.

'You know, I feel such a sense of urgency about all this. With some other Arab Christians I am working among the Arab churches to encourage them to have fellowship with our Jewish brothers. Today we have good relationships with many leaders of Messianic congregations in Jerusalem and other parts of the country . . . and we are trying our best to get to know more people and pastors so that we can have fellowship with them.

'There's a sense of hopelessness and despair in this country that Arabs and Jews can never live together. But I believe that God has called me to use my experience of learning to forgive to change this country of Israel; to show Jewish and Arab people, and indeed the whole world, that through Jesus, we can come together in peace and reconciliation.'

5

Father, Forgive!
– Olave Snelling

Olave Snelling has been working in the media world for many years – first in television, now in radio. Born in South Africa, just over sixty years ago, she enjoyed all the material benefits life could offer white people in those days . . . they lived well.

I have worked closely, in radio, with Olave for the past nine years, and when she heard I was involved in writing a book of stories of forgiveness with R. T. Kendall, she volunteered to tell me her story – a story of something that happened to her in childhood, that had only come to light recently and been dealt with.

It was an unfortunate experience at her privileged school that was to impact the life of this eleven-year-old girl for years to come.

Here Olave tells her own tale of total forgiveness:

' "Well, what are you going to play?"

'Nooooooo! This could not be happening. I was trembling

like a leaf. My heart was pounding. My chest was heaving. My eyes filled with tears. My legs turned to jelly.

'It was the school concert and, one by one, the pig-tailed, curly haired, bob-cut girls were stepping forward to play their party pieces. Suddenly in the midst of these procedures the headmistress called out, "Olave Cassidy".

'No. She had made a mistake. Didn't she know I had spoken with my piano teacher. She had told me, "You will be playing this Schubert piece at the school concert." "Oh," I had replied happily, "No, thank you very much. I can't do that. I can't play in front of people." I had smiled up at her cold and rather cross face, but as far as I was concerned that was the end of the matter. I would not be playing at the concert.

' "Olave Cassidy." The headmistress's voice rang out with that weight of authority that cannot be denied.

'Was she really saying that? Was she calling my name? I got up from my place and wobbled forward on unsteady legs.

'I approached the rather large and very black grand piano and looked down the length of the hall packed with girls from the entire school. As I stared down the middle aisle of what looked to me like the nave of St Paul's Cathedral, I saw at the end, seated on a scary large chair, the headmistress, Miss Le Maitre. Behind her on the wall hung enormous portraits of the two formidable founders of the school, Miss Lawrence and Miss Earle, who had carved this beautiful Sir Herbert Baker-designed building out of virgin bush in the early days of twentieth-century Johannesburg. It was the sister school of that other noble edifice on the white cliffs at Brighton in England – Roedean.

'Miss Le Maitre was not someone to be trifled with.

' "What are you going to play, Olave?"

'I stammered something, sat down at the piano, put my

hands on the keys, played about two bars, and the tears welled up. They then started to flow like Niagara in gushes of convulsive sobs. I pushed back the piano stool, got up from the piano on legs that felt as though they would collapse under me at any minute, and walked in as dignified a manner as I could out of the hall. I rushed up the stairs to the dormitory. By now I was racked with sobs and thought I was going to collapse. I started to feel dizzy and horribly sick and, after being found by matron, I was put in the sick bay. I started to vomit, and vomited continuously for four days. My head throbbed. My throat was constricted. The room was darkened. My eyes couldn't bear the light. If I moved my head a quarter of a centimetre, nausea engulfed me. I wanted the earth to open up and swallow me, and the bed if possible too, because I certainly couldn't think of getting out of it. I couldn't move. I couldn't think straight. I couldn't imagine ever feeling well again.

'A few days later – when back in school uniform and surprisingly still in one piece but with eyes like cannonballs from crying – as the bell rang and we clattered down the corridors to our lessons, I thought about how I could kill myself. I climbed up on to the window sill of the dormitory and looked down at the flagstones a long way beneath and tried to pluck up the courage to jump. But then I thought that maybe I wouldn't die; I might just end up being horribly mangled. It was a long way down. Obviously I didn't jump and life carried on. In fact, not a word was said by anyone about this incident ever again. I wondered why.

'In the days that followed I often re-ran the events of that day through my eleven-year-old mind: "But you *promised* I wouldn't have to play. Why did you do that to me, and humiliate me in front of the whole school?"

'From officialdom, no answer came. However, looking back, I now know the answer. I arrived at this august educational establishment absolutely thrilled to be going to the school to which my mother and sister went, to which my niece went (for a time), and to which my niece's cousins on the other side of my sister's family went. I was very eager to learn. I realised even at that age what a privilege it was to be there. It was a wonderful place of learning. It was also extremely beautiful, one of the most gorgeous school environments I've ever seen anywhere in the world. The food wasn't bad either. They did the best golden treacle pudding and the best fried bread ever.

'How could I ever trust anyone again? "She told me I didn't have to play," I said to myself. And I had believed her. How could my piano teacher have done such a cruel thing? Not to tell me that I was obliged to do what she told me, and then to suddenly find my name being called to play my silly little piece. I thought the piece I was working on at the time was pathetic. My mother had taught me piano from early on and, by the time I got to boarding school, I was tackling really difficult stuff and playing well.

'I had arrived bright-eyed and bushy-tailed for my first term at "big" school. I was a happy little girl with long blonde pig-tails. I came from a happy home in Maseru, Basutoland, where our father was an engineer – first of all for a private company and then for the colonial administration. My mother was a formidable person, a musical prodigy, with a volatile nature and temper to match. As I got into the swing of things at school, I looked at everything through the eyes of one who had enjoyed amazing freedom with my brother and sister and friends, galloping about on horses and living a gloriously free life. We had music at home pouring out of Mum on the

Bechstein grand: Chopin, Liszt, Bach, Beethoven in abundance, the songs of Schumann and Wolff, songs around the piano, two piano duets. We had outdoor activity, swimming, tennis, riding, gymkhanas, drag hunts, picnics in the mountains virtually every weekend, secure in the love of our parents, but also rigorous discipline, particularly from my mother.

'School, however, was rather a strange place. There was a mass of rules, most of which I considered to be trivial and stupid. If there was a good reason for a rule, it was perfectly rational to obey it. But if someone said only prefects could walk through a particular door, I would say to myself, "What's wrong with that door?" It didn't make any sense for just one category of person to walk through it, so I walked through it too! There was a path that only prefects could walk down, which was actually the shortest route to the gym. Well, if it was the shortest route, it didn't make any sense not to go down it. There was a bank on the front lawn which you couldn't run down unless you were a prefect, but I would run down it because it was much quicker to reach the lower part of the school. But that was not how things operated!

' "Olave Cassidy, take another Housemark. You aren't allowed to walk down that path."

'You were considered to be heinously dreadful if you got three Housemarks in one term. I received twenty-five Housemarks in my very first term! I didn't consider myself to be naughty at all. Just rational. But I was forced to think otherwise, constantly punished for my misdemeanours. But the punishments were so enjoyable that they didn't have any effect on me.

' "Learn this section of the 'Ancient Mariner' and come at Prefects' Tea tomorrow and recite that," said one Lord High Tomnoddy prefect. I did. I was very good at memorising and learning reams of poetry, so this presented no difficulty whatsoever.

' "Learn three pages of 'The Goblin Market' and come and recite it tomorrow at teatime." I did.

'I was given the prefects' stockings to darn. But I was really good at darning and did the most exquisite darns which I returned triumphantly with a sense of real achievement.

' "Go and clean Miss So-and-So's car," would come the command. I loved cleaning cars!

' "Go and collect pine cones for the music school fire." That was no problem at all. So in my second term at school when I told my piano teacher very politely (for there was never any question of being ill-mannered), "No, thank you very much. I can't play in front of people," I assumed that was that. She had said, "That's all right." But it wasn't.

★ ★ ★

'Fifty-one years later I found myself talking to Rosemary Phillips and a colleague from the Lazarus Healing Trust. We were praying over the previous generations of my family and I was confessing and endeavouring to deal with anything I knew about the "sins of the fathers" – anything in my past – in connection with prayer for healing of a persistent and painful condition. I've prayed for healing many times over the years and many people have prayed for healing for me. But now, once again, I needed to reflect upon what lay within me.

> Search me, O God, and know my heart.
> Try me and know my anxieties,
> And see if there is any wicked way in me,
> And lead me in the way everlasting (Ps. 139:23–4).

' "Is there anyone you need to forgive?" asked Rosemary.

'I had been asked this before, particularly when I first developed arthritis. There was a man in my church who always used to come up to me at the end of the service and say, "Have you been healed yet?"

' "No, not yet," I would say.

' "Why not?" he would ask.

' "Well, I'm not entirely sure," I would reply.

' "Do you have anyone you ought to forgive?" he would say. I had been over this territory many times before.

' "No," I would say. "I can't think of anybody I need to forgive."

'One day I particularly didn't want him to find me and ask the same question he had asked for months, so I hid behind a pillar. He found me.

' "Have you been healed yet, Olave?"

' "No, not yet." Then I had a flash of inspiration.

' "Do you know," I said, "One day I will die and one day you will die and we'll both die of terminal conditions. I think we're quits!"

'I thought hard for some minutes about Rosemary's question. I honestly couldn't think of anyone to whom I needed to extend forgiveness.

'But then, with appalling clarity, a picture flashed into my mind. There I was, aged eleven, standing by that dreaded grand piano at school. I instantly felt that terrible stab of nauseating humiliation, felt the clutch of let-down and betrayal from an uncomprehending adult world (or so it seemed), hell-bent on teaching me a lesson I would never forget.

' "When I was a child, I spoke as a child, I understood as a child, I thought as a child. But when I became a man, I put away childish things," says Paul in 1 Corinthians 13. How insightful! I thought that as a grown woman I had done that. Put away childish things. I thought when I gave my life to Christ as an eighteen-year-old I had forgiven everyone who, in my life up to that point, I needed to forgive.

'But I hadn't. This was the only person I had ever hated in my life. Oh no, not quite – I had heartily disliked a man for whom I worked in Christian television many years back. But I had long since let go of that, more particularly when he died under tragic circumstances many years later. No, there wasn't a trace of hatred left there.

'But my piano teacher had inflicted on me as a child what I thought was the greatest humiliation, a wound from which I actually felt incapable of recovering because the piano incident severely smashed through any confidence I had in my own abilities at a very deep level. That piano incident was the first and last time I played the piano to anyone but myself. Had I ever forgiven her? I suppose I had. But I couldn't remember consciously forgiving her as an adult. The incident was buried deep in my subconscious until that evening when it sprang vividly, fully formed, into my mind. My prayer for forgiveness towards this very small, roly-poly woman whom I hated was swift and came spilling out. I suddenly pitied her. That poor woman. Many teachers at our school were spinsters, the product no doubt of so many men having fallen in battle in the two world wars. I felt the pathos of their situation, year after year teaching us "gels" and pouring out their life's blood for us. What a life! It must have been very difficult to have pupils like me.

'But there was more to this episode than met the eye. My mother had been at Roedean. Indeed, she had been Head Girl for two years running. She was brilliant at music and went to study piano at the Royal College of Music in

London. There she was a contemporary of Malcolm Sargent (later Sir Malcolm), Benjamin Britten, Peter Pears, Arnold Bax, Imogen Holst, Richard Rodney-Bennett, Michael Tippett, Vaughan Williams, Moura Lympany. The list of luminaries of the music world went on and on. Then, in the crash of the world's money markets in 1929, her father lost his shirt, as did millions of others around the world. Mum had to return to South Africa to support her parents and took up a teaching job at the Johannesburg Roedean School. My teacher was there even then. She no doubt was envious of my mother when she announced her engagement to the handsome Charles Cassidy, who was an engineer working in Johannesburg. When I, the middle one of the three Cassidy children, bounced into the school many years later, what better opportunity to inflict some damage on this happy little girl who was rather inclined "to do it her way". At least so I thought.

'I thought of the words of the Apostle Peter: "How many times must I forgive?"

' "Seventy times seven," Jesus replied.

'Forgiveness is everything. Whenever he is talking to students, Dr Tony Campolo, a sociologist at Eastern University in the United States, asks what they would say sums up the Christian faith.

'Almost to a man, they say: "Love your enemies."

' "Yes," he says, "What else?"

' "Love your neighbour."

' "And then?"

' "Love your neighbour *as yourself*."

' "And *before* that?"

'It is that well-known summing up of the Law; what Jesus said when he was talking to the Pharisees, and one of them, a lawyer, asked him a question to test him: "Teacher, which is the great commandment in the law?"

' "You shall love the Lord your God with all your heart, and with all your soul, and with all your mind. This is the great and first commandment," said Jesus. "And a second is like it, You shall love your neighbour as yourself. On these two commandments depend all the law and the prophets" (Matt. 22:34–40, RSV).

'Love God with everything you are and with everything you've got. Love your enemies. Love your neighbour as you love yourself.

'Can we love our enemies? Can we love ourselves, truly and sincerely, let alone our neighbours. Our hospitals, clinics, psychiatric institutions, counsellors' practices and doctors' surgeries are stuffed to capacity with millions who hate or dislike what they are, and as a result suffer from depression, low self-esteem and manifest in their bodies what they feel in their souls and spirits. A doctor in our part of London told me that 70 per cent of the people they see in their practice have either stress-related illnesses or psychosomatic conditions brought on by what they feel. Not that the complaints aren't real, he added, they're brought about by what's happening internally.

* * *

'In 1899 my grandmother, Molly Craufurd, was on her way to visit her sister, Helen Buchan, in a place called Mafeking in South Africa. Her husband, Gordon, was an engineer who was building Cecil Rhodes's railway from Cape Town through the middle of the African continent to Cairo.

'To cut a long story short, the garrison town of Mafeking

under General Robert Baden-Powell was besieged by Boer troops. The siege went on and on and on, the horses from the Cavalry having to be slaughtered for food. My grandmother, and her sister, two of those amazing Victorian women who weren't aware they were doing anything particularly heroic, were enlisted to nurse in the hospital. I have in my possession her diary from the siege and some of the photo albums documenting this extraordinary time. For her bravery, fetching in both Boer and British wounded under fire, she was awarded the Royal Red Cross, the highest civilian honour possible, after the Relief of Mafeking and the lifting of the siege, an event that rocked Britain and the rest of the world to scenes of mad jubilation. Later she married my grandfather, Captain Edward Reading of the Canadian Cavalry, which marched up Africa alongside the pride of the British regiments to defeat the Boer armies. He was wounded and hospitalised in Bloemfontein where at a later date my grandmother met him.

'However, the British victory over the Boers did not end the conflict. It was at this point that the Boer guerrillas mounted a bitter and intense campaign against the British troops, swooping in on the armies under dead of night and inflicting atrocious fatalities. In order to cut the guerrillas off from their supplies, the British set out to implement a scorched earth policy. Boer homesteads and farms were burnt down, their cattle and crops destroyed, and the women and children put into camps (in fact, the first concentration camps in the world).

'The much-loved and respected Molly Craufurd was asked by General Baden-Powell to return from England to work on post-conflict reconstruction in South Africa. After her heroic efforts in the Siege of Mafeking, her kind of help was much needed. Little could she have known what lay ahead! It was the General's wishes that she bring her special touch to work in some of these camps.

'She loved and respected these Boer women and would do anything to help them. She got on very well with them in spite of not being able to speak their language. But disease was rife, particularly enteric and other fearful gastro-intestinal conditions. The main medication they had was Epsom Salts and the only means of preventing death was to deprive the ill of all but water and medication. They were accused of feeding the women cut-glass (for Epsom Salts looked like glass crystals) and of starving them to death. The Boer men used to creep into the camps under cover of night, bringing food, mainly coarse bread. The women and children would eat, and within a few hours would be dead from an internal haemorrhage because the coarse grain of the bread would rip open the thin walls of their intestines. These appalling scenes preyed on my grandmother's mind and she was remembering them even on her death-bed in 1951.

'My grandmother was loving those who were supposed to be her enemies. The very thing she was doing to save lives was construed as a policy of murder. How bitter is that? Could she forgive those who so misunderstood her and her motivation for what she had to do? Yes, I'm quite sure she could. I remember her as one of the most saintly people imaginable and I'm quite sure she would forgive, could forgive and did forgive, and go on forgiving. Could the Boer women and children forgive her and the British for the humiliation of defeat in a bitter war, for locking them up in concentration camps? I'm sure there were many who could and did – and yet there are many still alive today who find it difficult to forgive the English-speaking South Africans for the horrors their people suffered at the hands of the British over a century ago.

'Do as you would be done by? Love your enemies?

*   *   *

'Jesus was nailed to a cross for the love, compassion, mercy, kindness, healing and forgiveness demonstrated throughout his brief life and ministry. He was killed for restoring sight to the blind, movement to the lame, hearing to the deaf, for touching lepers and healing them, casting out demons and eating with tax collectors and sinners. At the moment of his greatest agony, he looked at the soldiers who had nailed him to the wood and said, "Father, forgive them, for they don't know what they are doing."

*   *   *

'In the grand scheme of things, it seems trivial to think of something that happened to me so long ago, and compare that in any sense whatsoever with the depths of forgiveness required over such wrongs as were wrought over decades of death, destruction and mayhem. But what the piano episode showed me is that forgiveness is specific to individual issues, especially if the Lord brings them vividly to mind as he did with me.

'I have come to the conclusion that there is only one way to forgive: to love God extravagantly with all my heart and soul and mind; to give myself totally to Christ; to love him for all I'm worth; and to paint my inner landscape with love. Then healing comes. I try to love myself because God loves me extravagantly. I ask God to help me love my neighbour as myself – even my piano teacher – and to speak well of those whom I consider to have spitefully used me long ago. It works!'

6

A Tough School
– Ray and Vi Donovan

Ray's and Vi's son, Chris, died at 3.30 a.m. on Saturday, 26 May 2001. He was murdered. The Donovans have learnt how to forgive the hard way. But even in the years leading up to this tragic event, their lives were punctuated by violence and trouble.

Ray is an Irish Londoner, and he used to drink a lot – as also did his wife, Vi, who was born in Bow. Their early married life was tough; fraught with arguments and strife. They had four children, but separated and divorced in 1977.

However, a year later they came together again and had two more children, Chris (born in 1982) and Phil (born in 1983), and for a while life improved. In fact, in April 2001 they actually remarried – a month before Chris died.

They found God just before Chris was murdered. Challenged by the words of Jesus in the Bible, they chose to forgive, publicly, the person who had committed this crime. And today they are helping other parents who have been bereaved, sharing their story of forgiveness with whoever will listen. This sort of forgiveness is costly, as you will see.

So, let's hear them tell their own tale of forgiveness, starting at the point of finding one another again after the divorce. How did that happen? Ray takes up the story:

'To tell the truth, for some reason that I have never properly understood, Vi's electricity was cut off and she came to me for help. We were divorced by this time, but I was so pleased she came to me for help. I loved them all so much. I wasn't going to leave them in the dark without any heating, so I suggested they all came back to stay with me. And that's what happened!

'There we were all together again, sat around the table having a meal. It was so good. Vi and I stayed up late that night and had a good talk; sometimes things got heated and we started to argue again. But then we would stop as suddenly as we started because we realised that we still both loved each other. It was a very healing time and the decision to re-marry each other was not a decision we took lightly. We'd argued for years. We used to drink a lot and tempers would get frayed. We would split up for a while, then get back together again; it had become a way of life. But on this occasion things were different. We weren't just getting back together for the sake of the kids this time – we were both making the decision to get back together for each other.

'So having been divorced, we started living together again and had two more children! What made the difference? Well, turning to God after my brother committed suicide.

'I'm from a large family and, over the years, we'd all gone our own ways and drifted apart. One day I got a phone call from one of my sisters to say that my mum had died. But there was something else she wanted to say and she told me to sit down. It was a big enough shock to hear my mum had died, but then she told me that the previous year my brother, Andy, had committed suicide.

'We'd been brought up to go to the Catholic church – occasionally. So I went up to the local church to light some candles and say a prayer. I was really upset that I hadn't known about Andy at the time it had happened; and with my mum dying too, I felt such a deep sense of loss. It really made me think and brought me to my senses. I didn't know how to grieve. What should I do? I lit two candles, then noticed the priest at the front of the church. I started to walk towards him. I really wanted to talk to him, tell him about my brother and my mother. But he ignored me. He turned away and walked in the opposite direction, and I was left standing alone in the church with grief being my only companion. It was getting dark and I felt very alone and very upset. Just when I needed some words of comfort and consolation, the priest ignored me. So as I walked out of that church I decided that I would never go into a church again.

'After we got together again, but before my mother died, we moved to Stoneleigh. There was a little Baptist church there and it was like a magnet – it kept drawing me. Every time I passed by, I wanted to go in, but I couldn't summon up the courage to enter. I was a hard man. I'd lived a rough life, and drinking and violence had punctuated my existence from childhood onwards. But as we settled into the neighbourhood I met a few people who belonged to the church. One was an elderly gentleman who, because he was crippled, drove to the church each week. I asked him if he would take me with him. I was so desperate to get into that church – but I was scared. I couldn't explain it, but there was something powerful about that place. I knew it was going to change my life, although I didn't know how.

'So here I was. My mother had just died, my brother had committed suicide the previous year and nobody had told me. I felt snubbed by the Catholic Church. We'd moved house and this Baptist church in Stoneleigh was starting to attract me. Things were happening to me that I seemed to have no control over. Vi found anything to do with "church" very suspicious; she didn't know anything about God – she hadn't had a Catholic upbringing like me.'

Vi took up the story:

'My only dealings with any "faith" happened when my sister got involved with a cult. She is still involved with these people, but genuinely believes that she is in a Christian faith. However, it *is* a cult, and it has been very destructive to the family because one day she walked out on her two teenage boys – just left them and went off with this group. So when Ray started talking about wanting to go to church, I was very frightened. I had known him since we were children. I knew what he was really like! And when he became a Christian, I got really scared and I thought I was going to lose him again. I watched as he started going to this church in Stoneleigh. I didn't want to go. He kept asking me to go with him, but I refused. I didn't want anything to do with those people because I thought they were brainwashing him!'

Ray continued:

'I was really attracted to this church. The more I went, the more I liked it. I think it was the friendliness of the people –

it had a good feel about it. I learnt about Jesus. In fact, I realised that you can talk to him. I experienced the Holy Spirit for the first time in my life; something happened inside me. Something was changing me – changing the way I behaved; changing the way I thought. I was no longer haunted by worry – I felt so peaceful. All the hurt I'd felt over losing my brother seemed to be healing. I wanted to know more – in fact, I was really *hungry* to find out more.

'I was sad when my mum died, but it was the death of my brother that really shocked me. Andy had always appeared to be so invincible. He was the eldest brother and the strongest in the family. We all looked up to him – in fact, we were all a bit afraid of him. He was the most vicious of the family. If you looked at him in a way he didn't like he'd hit you – hard. I never thought he'd be so weak as to . . .'

Ray's voice trailed off and he looked away. Tears filled his eyes. Even after the passing of time, he was still having trouble believing that his big brother had taken his own life. At first he hadn't understood what had pushed him to do such a thing, but then he met with his brother's children . . . and they showed him the suicide note that his brother had left. Ray continued:

'I then understood what had pushed him over the edge – he'd lost his wife. Ellen had died and he couldn't handle it. He loved her so much that he couldn't bear to live without her.'

We paused for a while. Grief was taking its toll on Ray. Perhaps the memories of Andy were merging with a more recent loss – a loss that was soon to happen to this family that had rediscovered itself and, as now, was undergoing a fundamental shift in its thinking:

'I used to think of myself as being a hard man. I respected Andy and liked to think I was like him. So when all this loss hit me and I felt so drawn to the church and found God, I had to persuade Vi that what I'd found was for her too. Shortly after Andy's death I started going to Stoneleigh Baptist Church regularly, and I joined an Alpha course. Each week I asked Vi to come too, but she refused. After a few weeks we reached the point in the course called the "Holy Spirit Day" and, much to my surprise, Vi agreed to come to that!'

Vi again took up the story:

'That's right, I deliberately didn't do the rest of the course. I was horrible to Ray; I would promise to go with him each week, but at the last minute I would refuse. I did it to torment him. I was trying to put him off. I was so unkind to him that he used to have to read the Bible in secret; sometimes I caught him reading it under the bedclothes! The problem was that I really thought I was losing him again. I was persecuting him because I was afraid. I thought that if I screamed and shouted and stamped my feet and made a fuss, he would change his mind. But the more horrible I was to him, the more loving he became towards me! I couldn't understand it. Sometimes he brought people home from the church and I would be awful to them. I didn't want these people in my house. I didn't trust them, and I thought they were taking my husband away from me. But they kept coming and they kept loving me and gradually I began to understand.

'So I went to the "Holy Spirit Day", having decided that if they were all totally mad then I would get up and walk out and drag Ray with me. At the back of my mind were the memories of what my sister had done to her family when she left them to join the cult. I sat there and listened. At first I thought a few of them were rather strange. I didn't really understand what they were talking about. They were describing the Holy Spirit and I didn't know anything about that. But as I sat there I began to realise they were just normal people. Then the pastor gave a talk and everything he said made sense to me. A few minutes later he encouraged the people to pray for their families and friends, in particular for those who were unwell. Now I'd never prayed in my life, so I didn't know how to! I lowered my head and said, "Lord, I am so scared, will you please help me," and I started to cry. I wept uncontrollably. I felt as though somebody had lifted a heavy weight off me. All the things I had been so concerned about – the worry over my sister and my concern for Ray – suddenly I understood. And the more I cried the more I understood; and I cried on and off for twenty-four hours. One minute I was laughing, the next I was crying! Ray had given me a Bible a few weeks previously that I had thrown against the wall in our bedroom. I went and found it and I read the parable of the lost sheep. I looked at Ray, and then I started to cry again. "That's me, isn't it?" I said.'

For Ray, these were surprising days:

'My mother had died, Vi and I were together again, I'd lost my brother, and now Vi and I were both Christians. Life had never been so changeable, but also so good. What we didn't know, though, was that we were about to be hit very hard.

'I came home from work one Friday evening. Phil was still out at work, but Chris was there and he made me a cup of tea and asked if I would drive him round to his sister's house in Streatham. I told him I was tired; I'd had a very busy week at work and all I wanted to do was sleep. We had a chat and laughed together, then he said he would go and visit some of his friends instead, and would meet up with Phil at around midnight when he finished work. So at around 6 p.m. he left and he kissed me on the forehead. It was strange, but the last words he said were, "I really love you, Dad." And with that he went out.

'We settled down for the night, watched a bit of television, and went to bed at around 10.30. Because they were going to a friend's house, we knew Phil and Chris would be out late. But very much later, at 1.30 a.m. on the Saturday, the doorbell rang. I went to the door to find two policemen outside. They said, "Can we come in?" I wondered what was going on and thought perhaps the lads had done something and they had been arrested – you think all sorts of things at times like this. One of the policemen told me there had been a fight and one of our sons had been seriously injured. We quickly pulled some clothes on and went with them in a police car, at great speed, to Epsom Hospital.

'When we arrived, a doctor came to speak to us. He told us that Chris had severe brain damage, his pelvis was fractured, his ribs were broken, his legs were badly injured – he was a complete mess.

'We later found out what had happened. Three of them had been walking down the road – Chris, Phil and a friend called Richard. They were on their way to another friend's house who happened to be a youth leader in another church. They were singing an Oasis song and a gang of nine people took a dislike to them and attacked them. From an eye-witness account, we later heard that they used Chris's head as a football; they took penalty kicks at it before running off and leaving him in the road. A car then came along and drove over him, before dragging him by his belt about forty feet down the road.

'We were numb and just sat there, praying for him in the hospital. After a short time we were taken to see Phil, who had also been injured but not so badly. His nose was broken and he was black and blue. Apparently they'd knocked him unconscious before starting to attack Chris. When Phil came round, he saw the car on top of Chris.

'We were told that Chris's life was in the balance and that he'd been rushed to the operating theatre. All we could do was sit and wait. We sat in a little room – it was like a cell. It was dingy and we were the only ones there. I got up, went out into the corridor and said, "Look, God, no matter what happens tonight, I'll always praise you."

'About twenty minutes later, the doctors came to see us and told us that Chris had died. That was the hardest moment of our lives. Then they asked us if we would like to see him. We followed them. The left-hand side of his face was completely bruised and kicked in and he still had a tube in his mouth. They didn't let us see anything from there down. Chris died at 3.30 a.m. on Saturday, 26 May 2001.

'Our pastor came to pray with us later that Saturday, and said, "I take it you won't be coming to church tomorrow." But I said, "You try and stop me. They took my son, they're not taking my faith, and they're not taking my most important thing, my joy."

'The church was fantastic. One of the guys said to us, "Jesus took your Christopher before he felt anything, do you know that?" I hadn't really thought about it, but as I started to think I thought, yes, you were there, you were there, God. And that thought took away the anger because I was angry with God at that time – I was *really* angry. I could go to church and praise him, but I was angry too. I couldn't quite understand why God, if he were there, allowed all this to happen. "Why didn't you stop it?" I would cry to him. But then I realised we don't understand, but God is in the midst of it.

'People often ask how we feel towards those young people who, we were told, were high on drugs and drink when they kicked Chris and attacked Phil. The truth is, we really feel for them. We feel sorry for them. I know it's hard to believe, but I feel such pity for them. Because of peer pressure and having to take the drugs and the drink, they are where they are now. They shouldn't be the ones behind bars; it should be the people who gave them the alcohol and the drugs. During the court case, when I heard them crying in the dock, I realised they were just children. I really do feel a lot of pity for them, which I know is something that God has put in me.

'Before the court case, I wondered how I would react. Would I be angry? Would I want to hit them, do something, shout and rant? I imagined all those scenarios. Actually, when it came to it, it wasn't anything like that. We had such inner peace. To be truthful, when we first saw them in court I did try to stare them out to make them feel uncomfortable. But then I had to close my eyes and say to Jesus, "I am so sorry I did that. I am so sorry."

'We found it in our hearts to forgive them. We *chose* to forgive them. We sat down and prayed and prayed; it didn't just happen – we did pray a lot.

'Chris died during a Bank Holiday weekend. We desperately wanted to see his body one last time. It was very hard for us because we had to wait until the Tuesday when the coroner took us to see our son. We kissed him on the forehead and said goodbye to him. As we stood there, gazing at Chris, the coroner said to us, "I am sorry to have to ask you this, Mr Donovan, but we need to remove your son's brain . . . we need to do some more tests to determine the exact cause of his death."

'The peace of God just came on me and I said, "That's all right. That's not my son lying there, that's just a carcass; my son is in heaven. You do what you need to do – it won't affect me at all now." And we went back to our pastor's house for lunch.

'Later that evening we went to our house group. It was there that I started to feel angry; I could feel the Peckham boy coming out. The group gathered round and prayed for me and – the Lord is so great – I heard Chris say, "Hello, Jesus." And the peace of God came on me again and then the joy of the Lord came in me and I couldn't stop laughing. I laughed for over an hour and twenty minutes. Real peace came into me that night and it hasn't left, it just gets stronger.

'In Matthew's Gospel it says that if we don't forgive, the Father can't forgive us. We *have to* forgive. I say to everybody, "God's not *asking* you to forgive, he's *ordering* you to forgive; you have to forgive." We can't go to church and raise our hands and pretend that we are all good Christians and not forgive. We've got to obey what the Lord says.

'As time passed, we wanted to use the experience of losing our son to help other families in similar situations. We shared our story in the press and on radio, and surprisingly we were told that the then girlfriend of one of the three boys who were found guilty of Chris's murder heard about our attitude of forgiveness towards them. She got in touch with our church, and we arranged to meet her. She told us that she had married her boyfriend, one of the murderers, in prison and he had heard about our feelings towards him and couldn't believe we had forgiven him. She told us that he would like us to visit him. He wanted to hear for himself what we had to say. We were all ready to go, but then everything was put on hold because there was an appeal coming up. The appeal took some time, and has only just happened (three years after the murder took place); but they lost it and so remain in prison. So now we are waiting to hear from the prison authorities as to when we can go and visit this lad.

'We've had a long time to think about this and we still want to go ahead and meet him. Nothing has changed. We're not the only family to have lost a son . . . four families have lost loved ones here. This boy needs to know he's forgiven. We're not above God, and if we say we're not prepared to forgive, then we're putting ourselves above God. And I know that if it were me in prison, I would be only too pleased if somebody came and told me they had forgiven me. He needs to hear about Jesus, and the love of Jesus, and if God can use me and Vi for that, then let him use us.

'The pain doesn't get any easier. But every morning, when we wake up, we ask the Lord to take our pain away. And forgiveness isn't just a one-off . . . every day we have to ask God to help us because the evil one puts thoughts in our minds and brings back memories that make us angry and upset . . . but when we pray, God takes it all away. We constantly battle with unforgiveness – it's a daily process. But after we have prayed, we're able to laugh and smile and joke and have fun – and a lot of people have come to the Lord as a result of our story.

'We now have our own ministry – it has slowly developed over the past two years as we told our story publicly on radio and television, and in the press. We go to local churches and tell people how to forgive. We take a suitcase with us that's handcuffed to our hands, and on the suitcase are the words

"Bitterness, Anger and Rage" – showing people what they drag around with them if they don't forgive. We've found that there is so much unforgiveness within the Christian Church. As we share our story, people come and ask us to pray for them. We were shocked at first by this lack of forgiveness – we were not expecting to find this in the Church. All we do is share our story . . . and it seems to challenge people and bring a great deal of healing. It means so much to us to see other people set free from unforgiveness . . . it's a joy that we can't describe.'

7

Abuse and Betrayal
– Evangeline Parmar

There is a saying, 'Life begins at forty'. This is certainly the case for Evangeline Parmar. Today she is a confident, attractive woman, who smiles a lot, holds her head high, and has a bounce in her step. You realise just how far she has come when you hear her story. It's a tale of abuse and betrayal. That she is who she is today is amazing, given all that she has been through in life.

To begin, Evangeline introduces us to her family and the world she grew up in; a situation that robbed her of all joy, and almost of life itself:

'We are a family of eight – my father, mother, three brothers, two sisters and me; I was their fifth child. We lived in a three-bedroom house in a nice area where everyone knew everyone else. In those days it was safe to leave your front door open; all the children in the neighbourhood used to play out in the street.

'It all started when I was five years old. I recall those times so well. We were taken to visit a friend of the family, and sometimes he invited us to stay the night. I can remember that while we were playing in his garden, he would be working in his garage, watching us from a distance. One day I was playing by the garage and he called to me, and beckoned me over. The next thing I knew he was doing sexual things to himself while I was made to watch. This went on for a few years and, as time went on, he became bolder; even when we were inside the house he would do the same thing and make me watch. Looking back, I didn't know then whether what he was doing was normal or wrong; I didn't understand what he was doing. I felt uneasy. I didn't like it, but I was scared to tell anyone – so I suppose I must have thought it was wrong. I really couldn't work it out.

'A few years later, when I was thirteen, someone tried to sexually abuse me but I fought him off. He threatened to kill me if I dared to tell anybody what had taken place between us. I was so upset at what happened that I told his family what he'd done. But they didn't believe me. I couldn't believe it. I felt so isolated, and so alone. And I was scared because I thought he might try to kill me. After all, if he had attacked me once, he might try again. So I made sure I was never alone with him. Even my own family thought I had lied! I couldn't believe that they would believe him rather than me, but they did.

'After that I started to smoke cigarettes. Life wasn't all that good at school. I tried to make friends, but because I wasn't very clever nobody really wanted to know me. I became depressed and, at the age of sixteen, I took an overdose. Looking back, I think I did it more for attention than anything else; I suppose it was a cry for help. I was taken to hospital and the doctors pumped me out, told me off, and sent me home.

'But as time went by, life didn't improve and I overdosed again at the age of eighteen. I just didn't feel loved or accepted by anyone. At home my mum was trying to make ends meet – my father had left her with six children to bring up on her own. Life was very tough for her. She worked all the hours she could to put food on the table, clothes on our backs, and pay the bills.

'In hindsight, it's easier to understand why I felt as I did. When I was a young child I can remember my father would often invite his friends over for a party. They would drink, dance and have a good time. We were always sent to bed as soon as the guests started to arrive, but we could hear what was going on and my dad was always the life and soul of the gathering.

'What I didn't fully realise at that early age was that he had a very bad temper and a very jealous nature. Apparently he used to accuse my mum of having affairs, and he used to beat her up until she was black and blue. But for years, while we were very young, she stood by him.

'But one day, when I was a little older, I witnessed him hitting my older brothers and sisters. By this time he often used to drink a lot and get very drunk, and then he would start lashing out at the family. At times like this I used to hide to avoid his flying fists.

'I later discovered that the truth was that it was he who was having the affairs, not my mum. More recently we found out that we have two step-brothers living in New Zealand somewhere; they are both older than me. My father once showed me a photo of them. And so it was that he left my mum when I was thirteen and went to live with the girlfriend he was having an affair with at the time.

'I then started hanging out with the wrong crowd, started smoking cannabis, and by the age of twenty I had become anorexic. That was because I found out that the only man I truly loved was having affairs with other women. I'm five foot, four and a half inches tall and was always underweight at the best of times, but due to the anorexia my weight dropped to under five stone. I used to look in the mirror and hate my reflection; I thought I was ugly and fat. I thought maybe if I lost some weight, then my boyfriend would stay with me and not go chasing other women. After mealtimes I would make myself sick. There were times when I would just eat one apple a day – if that.

'After eighteen months of starving myself I thought my body still hadn't changed enough – I still thought I looked fat. So one day I took a large quantity of laxatives and a short while later I collapsed. A doctor was called and they found the empty laxative boxes in the bin in my bedroom and once again I ended up in hospital. There I was weighed and they put me in a side room on my own, away from everyone else. Once again, I felt lonely. Out of sight from other people. Out of reach. Shunned and in disgrace. I was told that the only way I would be allowed to leave was if I started to eat and put on some weight.

'At the age of twenty-two I took another overdose. I had prepared this suicide carefully; this time I was not going to fail. Over several weeks I collected a vast number of different tablets, and by this time I was convinced that my life was meaningless. All I wanted was to love and be loved. But nothing changed. Nothing improved. I was used and then laughed at, so I just wanted to die. I thought I was better off dead than alive.

'This time I was taken to a London hospital (where they had a liver unit) as my liver was badly damaged because of all the paracetamol I had taken. I was in a coma for two days. I later heard that the doctors told my family I only had a 50 per cent chance of survival.

'I can remember being in that coma; it was as if I was falling down a well. I just kept on falling; there was nothing I could hold on to, nothing to break the fall. It seemed like a bottomless pit. It was cold and dark in there and I had this feeling that I shouldn't be in this place. Whatever was at the bottom of the well was bad and evil, and all the while I was falling, further and further. I looked upwards and I could see the sky at the top of the well, but the further I fell, the further away the light at the top seemed to get. Then all of a sudden I saw a hand appear from nowhere; I was still falling at the time. In my mind I thought that if only I could just touch the hand, I knew that I would be all right. With all my strength I tried to reach up towards the hand, and just as our fingers touched I woke up.

'And so I came out of the coma and stayed in hospital for a month or so. My family were told not to tell me that I had been in a coma – why, I don't know. But a few years later I asked a member of my family what had happened to me in hospital . . . and it was then that they told me how close I had come to dying. Some time after that I started dabbling with the occult. But it wasn't long before the "dabbling" became more serious and I found myself getting deeper and deeper into things I shouldn't have been doing . . . all because I so wanted to be loved.

'At that time of my life I would have done anything to hold on to the man I loved! There were a couple of people I knew who asked me if I had ever visited a witch doctor, and of course I said no. I didn't even know that they existed in this country, that's how naive I was. However, they told me that if I had money they could take me to see this man and he would do or give me something that would force my boyfriend to fall in love with me! And so I found myself going from one witch doctor to another. I didn't care what I had to do; it seemed as if getting my boyfriend to fall in love with me was my mission in life – I literally worshipped the ground he walked on. Of course, none of it worked; these people just took my money and played on my emotions.

'I must admit, while I only loved this one man, even though he would come and go in my life throughout the years, I did have other boyfriends. I thought perhaps I could find love elsewhere with somebody else, but that wasn't to be.

'In December 1997 I was going through a very hard time in my life. I was so consumed with hurt feelings and painful emotions that I just couldn't think straight and move forward in life. Nothing was improving. I was still seeing the same boyfriend, on and off. By this time we had two children, but it had taken me four years to track him down after I conceived with our youngest child. I was convinced that if he knew about the pregnancy, he would be a father to two children, he would come and live with us, and settle down. I needed to find out if he wanted to have a relationship with his children.

'When he told me he didn't know how to be a father, and he didn't want to commit to them, my eyes were finally opened. At that moment, I realised I no longer wanted to live a life based on false promises, because that's all he ever gave me. Now, being a mother, I didn't want any of my children living on false promises, having their hopes raised, then dashed to pieces. So I told him I'd had enough of his lies and I didn't want to know him any more. He was shocked; he never thought I would stand up for myself. But that day I did, and I've never looked back.

'I realised that all my life people had walked over me. But now things were different. For the sake of my children, I would not allow this to happen to me any more. These children looked up to me; they needed a mother who would take care of herself as well as them.

'Even before I had my children, I tried to get my life in order. I stopped meddling with the occult, and I stopped hanging around with the people who were a bad influence on me. I used to pray to God to give me a child, and by the time I had my first baby, I had moved away from most of my past life – my so-called friends. I started going to church occasionally. When my second child came into this world, I started feeling more and more content with my life – for a time.

'In February 1998 my life was to change completely. I met a Christian friend and we talked about God. I told her I'd always known he was there, but I never knew how to have a personal relationship with him. She talked to me and tried to answer all my questions, and on 4 February 1998 I committed my life to the Lord Jesus; I handed control of my life and the lives of my children over to him. I felt an enormous sense of relief that everything would now be all right.

'Today I can look back with hindsight and see how Jesus has changed our lives in such a wonderful way that there's no turning back for us. He has taught me the real meaning of love; and how to love. No longer do I have to give up my body in return for love.

'My walk with the Lord has taught me to be patient and the importance of being obedient to him. It has been six years since I have become a Christian, and the truth is that there have been times when I've wanted to walk away from the Lord! You see, I was a completely broken person. All my life the people that I trusted abused me, rejected me, or left me. The man I loved most was the one who rejected me more than anyone else. But God was so gentle and patient with me that I didn't know how to deal with it. When I started reading the Bible, the Lord spoke to me through this scripture: Deuteronomy 31:6. It says, "Be strong and courageous. Do not be afraid or terrified because of them, for the Lord your God goes with you; he will never leave you nor forsake you."

'As I started trusting God more, another scripture spoke to me: Jeremiah 18:6. This says, "Can I not do with you as this potter does? . . . Like clay in the hand of the potter, so are you in my hand."

'Then after a while God started talking to me about forgiveness. I read another scripture: Isaiah 1:18. This says, " 'Come now, let us reason together,' says the Lord. 'Though your sins are like scarlet, they shall be as white as snow; though they are red as crimson, they shall be like wool.' "

'I asked the Lord what he meant by this, and he told me that he had forgiven me, washed me clean in Jesus's blood, and now I had to forgive myself! The problem was, I didn't *want* to let go of my past hurt, because that was all I'd ever known. I had become so accustomed to those emotions they had shaped my personality and made me the person I was. In fact, I had been like that for most of my life, since the age of five, so I didn't know any different. I thought that if I started to think differently, then I would become a different person – I would lose my identity and become somebody I didn't know. Then the Lord spoke to me from Psalm 32:8, "I will instruct you and teach you in the way you should go; I will counsel you and watch over you."

'It took a lot of tears as I had so much anger and resentment to deal with; so much hurt inside of me. I thought it would never end. Weeks and months passed and slowly, bit by bit, God chipped away, and each time I gave a memory over to him, he would heal me in that area. And then, finally, I was able to forgive myself. And when I did, I felt such a release it was awesome. I also understood what God means when he says, ". . . the peace I give you surpasses all understanding".

'When I reached this point, I felt so much joy and happiness enter my life that I couldn't contain it! I felt I wanted everyone to have it! So I started praying for all my family and friends to be saved. (And I still do.) But I hadn't reached the end of the healing process.

'I was talking to the Lord one day and during our time together he told me I needed to start forgiving each and every person who had hurt me in the past. I said, "Lord, I thought I'd given it all over to you?" And he said, "You have, my child, and you have learnt to forgive yourself. Now you need to forgive the people who did all those things to you." I replied, "But that's your job, isn't it?" He said, "It is not for you to judge them."

'This was new to me and I didn't know how I was going to do this. As I continued to read the Bible, searching for answers to these questions, I discovered this scripture: Romans 8:14–17: ". . . those who are led by the Spirit of God are the sons of God. For you did not receive a spirit that makes you a slave again to fear, but you received the Spirit of sonship. And by him we cry, 'Abba, Father.' The Spirit himself testifies with our spirit that we are God's children." Romans 8:28 helped me too. It says, "And we know that in all things God works for good to those who love him, who have been called according to his purpose."

'I said to God, "OK, I'll do this, and I'll trust you that these people will not be able to hurt me again." Forgiving the first person was easy because he was already dead, so I forgave him in my heart. As for the person who attempted to abuse me at the age of thirteen, that was more difficult; I didn't know where he was. So I forgave him in my heart. However, some time later I was at a social gathering and I saw him. Normally I greet people with a hug, so I went right up to him and looked him straight in the eyes and said, "Hello." Then, in front of his family, I gave him a hug. Again I felt that release in my spirit.

'Later, I telephoned the father of my children and spoke to him for a long time and then asked him to forgive me. He said there was nothing to forgive, but I told him about the things that I'd done – things he'd not known about. And he forgave me. That was when I told him I had forgiven him for all the years of heartache he had put me through, as well as our children. As soon as I started to forgive all the people who had hurt me, I prayed to God for their salvation.

'There was also a time when the Lord gave me an opportunity to see my dad, and for the first time I can remember, I felt pity for him. None of his children wanted to know him after the way he had treated our mother and us. I now had the boldness to ask him the questions I had wanted to ask him for years. Why had he treated our mother like that? Why did he leave us? And why did he never tell me that he loved me? And it was the last question, about him never telling me that he loved me, that was why I guess I always felt unloved. Being a mother myself now, I know how important it is to always let my children know they are loved and appreciated. And when I asked my dad why he had never told us he loved us, he just wept. As he wept, I so wanted to hear him say that he loved me, but he couldn't bring himself to say those simple words. I told him that I loved him because he was my dad, and also because the Lord says in his word that we must always honour our mother and father. A member of my family told me that when my dad was growing up, his parents never told him that they loved him. But in that moment, I felt he still could have told me what I wanted to hear. I also knew I still had to forgive him for all the things he put us through when he was with us.

'When I eventually forgave him, that's when I was finally able to accept that God was my Father in heaven. You see, I didn't really know what it was like to have the love of an earthly father when I was growing up, because he left us when we were young. And I couldn't accept God being my Father until then. Before that, when I prayed, I used to say "God" or "Lord"; I always found it difficult to call God "Father". Now, because I don't see God through the experience of my earthly father, I know God the Father loves me unconditionally!

'I've also taught my children that even though their biological father doesn't want to know them, our Father in heaven loves them no matter what. I've also told them not to hate their dad – just to forgive him, and release him to the Lord. I have also told them that only God knows if he will ever bless me with a husband, and a father figure to them.

'As I was reading my Bible recently, the Lord spoke to me through Jeremiah 39:17: " 'But I will rescue you on that day,' declares the Lord; 'you will not be handed over to those you fear. I will save you; you will not fall by the sword; but will escape with your life, because you trust in me,' declares the Lord."

'Through the years I have known God, some of my brothers and sisters in the Lord have offended me, and I too have offended them; most of the time not deliberately. Sometimes we can all rub people up the wrong way; sometimes we don't even know that we have done such a thing! When these things happened to me in my early walk with the Lord, I used to take offence at every bad word that was spoken against me. Inside it would eat me up and I would be so angry towards that brother or sister. I didn't realise that I could go up to them, and tell them how I had felt about those things they had said to me, and try to sort things out. Instead I used to cry to the Lord, and ask him what I should do. And every time he told me to forgive them. I used to argue with God and say to him, "But this time it wasn't my fault" or "They started it first!" And he still always told me to forgive. At that time I didn't know that in the Bible, when Peter asked Jesus what he should do if his brother sinned against him, Jesus told Peter to forgive not just up to seven times, but up to seventy times seven. And I'll be honest, I didn't always do it straightaway. But I found the longer I left it, the more resentment I had towards that person. But I wasn't Miss Perfect! God was doing his work in me – by teaching me that it's OK, he understands how I feel, and not everybody is the same as the people I have known in the past.

'When I started being obedient to the Lord and started forgiving even my Christian friends, I would feel such a release and my heart would change to have love and compassion towards the person I had a grievance against. Sometimes I would feel it wasn't fair, but I would forgive because

God tells me to. He knows all things, his thoughts are not our thoughts, and his ways are not our ways.

'I can remember a couple of years ago, my youngest child came home from school in tears. I asked her what was wrong and she went on to tell me that her teacher had been in a foul mood and had shouted at the class all day long. He had apparently upset most of the children in the class. So I told my daughter that maybe he'd had a bad night or was tired, and he probably didn't mean to get so angry with them. The next day we prayed together for this teacher and asked God to forgive him for upsetting the children in the class; also, my daughter asked God to soften this teacher's heart towards all the children in the school. (This was the only teacher in the school who made the children feel afraid.) My daughter was all smiles going to school that day, hoping that her prayers had been answered. Well, all I can say is, one look at the teacher's face completely wiped the smile from my daughter's face. Every day she would come home more and more upset, crying that she didn't want to go to school any more because of her teacher's rudeness and hostility towards the class.

'This went on for months – I even tried talking to him myself and asked him if anything was wrong. He said everything was fine. And all the while I was teaching my child that, no matter what, she must forgive her teacher and release him to the Lord. We prayed day and night for this teacher, and I also got one of my prayer partners to pray with me about the situation. By now, a few of the other parents were starting to get quite upset about this teacher too. Then one day he left the school, and we all received a letter from the headteacher saying that, for a long time, this teacher's father had not been well and he was now leaving to look after him. The following

term, this teacher returned to the school and we discovered
that his father had had cancer and died.

'The reason I have added this story is to let you know that
my children and I were taught a valuable lesson through this
trying experience: that we don't always know why people
hurt other people, but it could be that they are hurting
themselves, and they don't know how to express their feelings.
So the only way they know how to react is to lash out at
others, although I know that this doesn't excuse the way this
teacher treated the children in the school.

'But I thank God we have him in our lives because he
gives us that deep inner compassion and love towards people.
Whenever my children or I are going through tough times,
like my daughter did at school, I always quote Daniel 3:25 to
them, to remind them that no matter how bad the situation
is, Jesus is always walking with us through the furnace: "Look!
I see four men walking around in the fire, unbound and
unharmed, and the fourth looks like a son of the gods."

'There have been times in my life that I have had to ask
my children to forgive me. For example, I would say something like, "Listen, I'm your mother and I know that I am
right." And I would be so adamant, only to find out later that
I was giving them the wrong answer! And they would have
this smug look on their faces to say, "Come on, Mum, we're
waiting, would you like us to forgive you now, or shall we
wait until you say you're sorry?!" And of course I always ask
them for forgiveness, and we laugh it off. Also, there have
been times when I have had to tell them off for not listening
to me and have sent them to bed. Then, the next morning
my youngest daughter will, nine times out of ten, come up to
me and say, "Mummy, I forgive you for being angry with me
yesterday!" '

8

The Brighton Bomber
– Harvey Thomas

Given that he's an international public relations consultant and counts Margaret Thatcher and Billy Graham among his clients, it is perhaps a sign of his highly original, no frills and financially canny attitude that the subject of this chapter works out of what looks like a lock-up garage on a light industrial site in Potters Bar.

You have to squeeze through the door, past a bookcase overflowing with paraphernalia, and there, at the end of a short corridor, is the welcoming, affable Harvey Thomas, CBE.

A large man, he sits behind an equally large desk piled high with video tapes, books, computer screens and telephones. On the walls hang pictures of Harvey Thomas – with 'Mother' (Margaret Thatcher), with Billy Graham, with John Major, and did I notice Harvey with the Pope?

'Coffee?' he asks. And no sooner said than done, his wife, Marlies, who obviously anticipates his next suggestion before it has passed from his lips, brings in two mugs of coffee with a plate of digestive biscuits.

'I can't eat those,' he says, 'I'm on a diet!' But it doesn't seem to make any difference!

I must confess, I was expecting to see him in far more illustrious surroundings, given his reputation. But this is where he's worked for many years and, let's face it, he's been very successful doing so. Harvey's website says it all: 'Public Relations and Personal Adviser to Presidents, Prime Ministers and World Leaders – Harvey Thomas has been responsible for planning, staging and presenting thousands of Conferences and Promotional Events in over 100 Countries.'

However, his loyalty to Margaret Thatcher and the Conservative Party almost cost him his life because in the early hours of 12 October 1984 the IRA detonated a bomb that devastated the Grand Hotel in Brighton, where leading members of the Conservative Party were staying during their party conference. Harvey, one of the conference organisers, was five feet from the blast.

He survived. More recently, his faith in God and his belief in the Bible challenged him to forgive the man who masterminded the bombing – the notorious Patrick McGee. In fact, he's done more than that. Harvey has become good friends with Patrick McGee and has even shown him hospitality in his own home with his wife and daughters.

I visited Harvey to hear the story of how he has forgiven and befriended the person who nearly robbed him of life, Marlies of her husband, and their daughters of their father. But this is one story that Harvey never intended to be published, and that it leaked out into the public domain a few years ago was not his intention. For Harvey, his story of forgiveness was meant to be a matter between him, the man who tried to kill him, and God.

To understand what and who have shaped Harvey, you have to understand the course his life has taken. In some respects he's a maverick. His father wanted him to become a solicitor, but after starting a degree in law, he gave it up because, he told me, 'I'm a talker; solicitors sit behind desks and I don't!' So having disappointed *his father, who was himself a barrister, what did he do? Harvey takes up the story:*

'In 1960, when I was twenty, I started working with the Billy Graham Evangelistic Organisation on the North of England Crusade that was to be held in Manchester. It happened because I knew a guy called Maurice Rowlandson. At that time, Maurice was a youth leader at a church in north London; he also worked for the Billy Graham organisation in the United Kingdom. I told him I was looking for something to do and he said, "Well, I am looking for someone to organise the sound landline relays out of Manchester." '

Despite never having done anything like that in his life, Harvey grabbed the opportunity that proved to be the start of a long liaison with the Billy Graham Organisation, taking him to Minneapolis, then Honolulu, where he became involved in radio and television. He later became the press officer for the World Congress on Evangelism in Berlin in 1966, and from 1970 to 1975 he was the Director of Billy Graham's crusades around the world.

'By 1975 I felt that I had really done enough of that kind of thing, so I became an independent consultant in 1976. I did all sorts of projects in Saudi Arabia, South America and various other places.

'I had gained incredible experience working with Billy Graham. Setting the example himself, Billy rightly expected us to match the world's standards in what we did, while at the same time maintaining an uncompromising Christian testimony. It was a steep learning curve and I came out of it with a huge experience of working internationally. By the end of my time with Billy, I had worked in over one hundred countries with him. I set up all the committees for the International Congress on World Evangelisation in 1974, which meant going round the world four times, and visiting eighty-five countries in order to bring the right people together. I met my wife, Marlies, at that conference and we married in 1978. We then had two daughters who were born in 1984 – five days after the bomb attack – and 1986. They are both gorgeous.

'While on my way home from South America in late 1977, I spent a day in Dakar, in Senegal in West Africa, because I had arranged a stopover there to break the journey from Rio to Frankfurt. When I went through passport control at about three in the morning, I had to look up – despite being six foot four tall – at two very, very black African gentlemen who had very white teeth! All I could see was their teeth because there was very little electric lighting in Dakar airport in those days. To my surprise, they looked at my passport and laughed. I asked them what they found so funny and they said, "Well, it says Great Britain, but Britain isn't so great any more."

'I thought about this. I had been out of England for fifteen years, except for a few days each year when I would stop over on my way to somewhere else. As I looked at my country with fresh eyes, I came to the reluctant conclusion that, in my opinion, Britain had no viable government. Jim Callaghan was Prime Minister and living in Number 10. The Labour Party was theoretically the government, and since they appeared to me to be totally incapable of doing anything whatsoever, I thought I probably belonged to the "other side".

'So I went to Conservative Central Office and offered to help them for a while. I thought I ought to do my bit for my country because I had been living in America and elsewhere around the world while England was crashing down. When I went to see them and they said, "What do you do?" I showed them a photo of a packed Wembley Stadium and that was basically that. They asked me to stay for six months and offered me a nominal honorarium which I agreed to. Then came the election of 1979 in which I organised much of Mrs Thatcher's election tour and stage-managed all of her big meetings and rallies. I arranged a large meeting at the Wembley Conference Centre, where we introduced, for the first time, people from the world of showbusiness who were sympathetic towards the Conservative Party. It was after this event that Margaret said to me, "Will you stay on and work with me as my adviser?" So I stayed with her for over thirteen years. I staged all the party conferences. I looked after the press, the media and the broadcasting, and when she retired she very kindly gave me a CBE. I worked fourteen hours a day, and that was the role in which I was attending the Brighton Conference in 1984 – I was actually the director of the conference. I was responsible for the room assignments, so I put myself in Room 729 on the top floor of the hotel.'

As we sat in his office, Harvey showed me a photograph of the Grand Hotel in Brighton taken a few hours after the bomb had ripped through the heart of the building. I could see how the floors had collapsed one on top of the other. Then he played a video of the television news reports of that fateful day:

'That was the room I was in. I was there, and the bomb was there, five feet away. I was blown up through the roof, down three floors, and my body caught on a girder just below the fifth floor. Ten tons of rubble fell on top of me, but they dug me out two and a half hours later completely unhurt.'

I watched the video as the firemen discovered his body . . . his eyes sealed closed against the dust; he was hardly distinguishable, his face covered in a pale-grey powder from the masonry rubble in which he'd been entombed.

'I was conscious the entire time and for the first few minutes I had no doubt at all that I was going to die. I was flung into the sky before crashing through the roof of the Grand Hotel; bounced down through three floors, and came to rest before piles of rubble came crashing on top of me. I could hear the firebells ringing in the distance, their sound fading as more and more rubble fell on me. Then icy cold water started to pour past my face because the pipes had been fractured in the blast. I had no doubt then that I was going to die.

'When everything settled and I was totally buried – I was lying on my back with my hands covering my nose and mouth – I couldn't move anything. I was totally encased in rubble. I could feel a nail had pierced my left foot; it was very painful.

'But if I died, I knew exactly where I was going, so it wasn't me I was worried about. However, Marlies was five days overdue with Leah (our elder daughter), which was why she wasn't with me – usually she came everywhere with me. Marlies wouldn't have survived being blown up but, as the fireman said to me, "Your substantial bulk saved you."

'When they rescued me, two and a half hours later and after a lot of digging, I was finding it hard to breathe because the water was occupying all the holes in the rubble on top of me. I was trying to call for help, but I couldn't take a deep enough breath to shout loudly. Then I heard someone say, "Quiet, quiet, I can hear something down there." They had heard my muffled calls for help. I remember thinking how grateful I was to be English and not French, as I didn't have to think about which tense to shout in. It's funny what goes through your mind at such times!

'I was surprised to be alive because when I was being hurtled through the sky after the bomb went off, I really thought that I was going to die and remembered a verse in the Bible, "If we confess our sins he is faithful and just to forgive us our sins and cleanse us from all unrighteousness" (1 John 1:9). And I can vividly remember saying to the Lord that if I had any sins left unconfessed, "Would you mind taking them as read as I haven't got a lot of time right now!" I had rubble all over my eyes, I couldn't even open them – it was just muck and rubble and dust and wet.

'So eventually the firemen dug me out and I asked them, "Where are we?" They said, "Below the fifth floor." So I told them that I could walk down the stairs and out of the hotel from there, but they would not allow me to do that because they were afraid I might have internal injuries. A doctor came up on a cherry picker and asked if I wanted some painkillers, but I declined his offer as I could feel my toes and hands. The firemen insisted on putting me on a stretcher and carrying me down to ground level; it took seven of them to carry me down the stairs. They said if they had known what I weighed, they would have gone and rescued someone else!

'And so I was put in an ambulance and taken off to hospital for a check-up. I was almost the last to be rescued. The Tebbits and John Wakeham came out after me – they were terribly injured.

'The doctors at the hospital confirmed I didn't have any broken bones, they gave me a tetanus jab, and I took about six baths – so much rubble came out of my body that the nurse had to scoop it out of the bath with a dustpan and brush. I was desperate to let Marlies know I was alive, so when I got to the hospital I asked someone to phone her and say, "Harvey's fine, he'll call you himself."

'Eventually I spoke to Marlies; my mother was with her by this time and I said, "Please get down here, I've got no clothes to wear!" So despite being five days overdue, she caught the 7 a.m. train down from London. The thing she remembers most is that when she got to Brighton – and remember this is a nine-and-a-half-months pregnant woman and a seventy-eight-year-old woman – the journalists just shoved them out of the way and wouldn't let them get to the taxis; the press had come down from London to Brighton on this train having heard about the bomb, and they wanted to get to the bomb site first.

'Finally, they arrived at the hospital with a set of clothing for me, by which time I was getting cleaned up. I had given some television interviews, which I had to do because other people were more badly injured than me. So then I put my clean clothes on, discharged myself from the hospital, and went back to run the conference.

'Knowing Margaret Thatcher, I had assumed that she would want it to be business as usual. So I had phoned my secretary and warned her that I would be late because of the bomb, ". . . but," I went on, "I know that 'Mother' will want to go on time, so get down there and do all the checklists." So she went off and did all the standard checklists and got the technical boys organised. Only later did I see the interview that Margaret did with John Coles, "The conference will go on as usual. Did you get that, John, the conference *will* go on."

'And so I was back in the conference hall at 9.30 a.m. and it was only then that I realised the full extent of what had happened the night before.

'The shock never did set in; it didn't have a chance really because I was running the conference that day. I went to see "Mother" in the hall and we decided not to use the autocue. She was preparing to give a speech in the afternoon so we reworked it in the morning. She gave the speech, and everybody cheered. Marlies and my mother were sitting at the back; we stayed in Brighton that night and then we drove back to London the next day. Then I began to feel the bruising, because I had been pretty battered. Yes, by this time I was feeling very, very battered and bruised – but fine.

'Five people were killed in the bomb blast. They asked me in an interview how I felt towards the terrorists who had carried out the bombing. I said, "If anything I feel a bit guilty because if we in the Christian Church were a little more passionate in passing on our faith, we probably wouldn't have so many terrorists."

'As time went on, Patrick McGee was caught, tried, and found guilty of the Brighton bombing. Two other people committed this bombing with him, but nobody knows who they are and I haven't asked him. I have discussed it with him, but I haven't asked him.

'In 1998, fourteen years after the Brighton bombing, I attended an international conference to do with reconciliation. It was held in Louisville, in Kentucky, and I was there leading the European delegation. I had belonged to this movement for quite a while and the conferences took place every two or three years with delegates coming from all over the world to tell their stories of reconciliation within the Christian Church and family: Protestants, Catholics, black, white, young, old, inter-denominational – a range of stories from a range of backgrounds.

'It suddenly dawned on me that here was I talking about

reconciliation, talking about forgiveness, and that actually I had taken no steps in my life at all to make any contact with the IRA or the person who put the bomb under my bed in the Grand Hotel in Brighton. For the first time since the bombing, I realised I was talking about forgiveness but not doing anything about it. So I prayed about it, and talked to Marlies, and I knew very definitely I had to take a step in that direction. So I wrote to Patrick McGee in the Maze prison and told him that as a Christian I felt I ought to write and say that I forgave him for the thing that he had done; that I could only speak on my own behalf, not on the behalf of anyone else, because I didn't have the right to do that. So, I wrote, "I forgive you." And that was that. I didn't tell anybody else — only Marlies knew I had done this.

'He wrote a very nice letter back; he's actually a Doctor of Philosophy from the University of Coleraine, a highly educated man. He'd had a very tough life and joined the IRA after Bloody Sunday when he had decided, "Enough is enough. If this is how we are going to be treated by the British government . . . They have treated us abysmally for 200 years . . ."

'And in a sense, he was absolutely right — we had treated the Catholics and Nationalist sympathisers in Ireland absolutely appallingly — but of course, I do not believe that in any way justifies violence. They couldn't get jobs; they couldn't reach a senior level in the Royal Ulster Constabulary. They couldn't really do anything. I think it was appalling how we treated them. So after he replied to my letter, I went to see him in Dublin after he was let out of prison in 2000 — a year later. We met in the back room of a house belonging to a friend of his, a lady called Anne Gallagher, who runs a reconciliation programme called "Seeds of Hope", and we sat and chatted for four or five hours.

'I liked him and am now a patron of his work for restorative justice and reconciliation in Ireland. He is finding it tough going because he's trying to bring together victims of crime with the perpetrators of the crime. He's doing it very sensibly. He's doing it his way. But my motive for meeting him was different. I believe that the Bible teaches you to forgive. And that's it.

'I suggested he came over to England where I could help him in talking to the media about his project. So he flew over one Saturday morning. Leah, my elder daughter, who was by then seventeen, came out to the airport to meet him and we went back home for breakfast. Lani, my younger daughter, who was born two years after the bomb, was at home, and she said to Patrick at the breakfast table, "You do realise that if you had succeeded in killing Daddy, I wouldn't be here."

'So we had breakfast, shared a long day together, and we have since become good friends. I know he is sorry that his actions have caused hurt, injury and death. He still believes that there was no alternative, at that time, to declaring war on the British government. While I, on the other hand, totally disagree with him on that issue, the fact remains that in historical terms, history sadly shows us that violence works. Had there been no violence in Ireland, we would still be treating Catholics and Nationalists abysmally. I do not believe that this fact excuses the violence; I am simply trying to understand why these things happen as they do.

'Yes, he was surprised that I had forgiven him. He couldn't understand it at first. I think he does now as we have come to know each other well and we keep in touch regularly. And yes, he has apologised. He has said again and again that he is really sorry that he had to be involved in violence and that he caused hurt, injury and death, but he felt that there was no other option at that time – not to try and kill us, but to try and attack the British government.

'So what difference did the process of forgiveness make to me? Well, it was a decision I myself took and some people disagreed with me. Peter Hitchins, in the *Sunday Express*, said, "Who does Harvey Thomas think he is?" To which I wanted to reply, "I'm the guy who got blown up. I've a right to forgive!" But I didn't mind Peter Hitchins's comments at all. It doesn't matter to me what other people think, because it was clearly something that I believed I had to do. I didn't suddenly hear a voice from heaven, but it was quite clear that God was speaking to me through the other speakers at that conference on reconciliation, and I realised I had no option but to say "I forgive". I have no criticism of anybody who doesn't feel as I do. Others suffered far more than I did in the Brighton bombing.

'When the story about me meeting with Patrick McGee leaked out a couple of years later (and I still don't know how that happened), the *Evening Standard* called me one day to say they had heard I'd been in touch with the "Brighton bomber", and was it true that I had written to him to say I'd forgiven him? I told them that yes, it was true. They wanted to know why they hadn't heard about it! I told them it was none of their business!

' "Is it secret?" they wanted to know.

' "No, it's not secret, it's just that some things are private," I replied.

'I keep praying for Patrick McGee. He has a wife and some young children. He's finding it very tough.

'Forgiving him is something I decided I had to do; no doubt in my mind, I had to do it.'

9

The Fruit of Forgiveness
– Melissa Clark

Today Melissa Clark (this is not her real name – to respect the privacy of her family, we have changed her identity) is working in Argentina with underprivileged children and their families. Melissa's parents come from two different countries and, as a consequence, she is bi-lingual. She is the eldest child in the family, and has two brothers.

When she was eighteen, Melissa went abroad to work as an au pair for a while. She returned to the United Kingdom and was persuaded by many people to go to university; but she hated it, and stayed for just five weeks before leaving. After this, she found work in hotels, and then was offered a job abroad, where she stayed for seven months before leaving to travel for three and a half months with a friend. When she was twenty, Melissa found another job working in a luxury hotel.

'The only reason I was working there,' she told me, 'was because I was running away from home; my parents had just got

divorced and I was full of anger towards my dad.' Melissa takes up the story:

'The trouble at home started when I was sixteen, and two years later my dad left. There was a bitter court battle between him and my mum and I took a lot of days off school to support her because she didn't have anyone else to talk to. I was the one she confided in. I used to go with her to court but kept out of sight because I didn't want my dad to see me. I didn't want to hurt him. His hair was all over the place; he looked like a wild man. They said he had schizophrenia, but I don't actually believe in those illnesses – I think that sometimes society today finds it a convenient excuse to attach labels to people when we can't cope with the way these people are acting. I now believe that my dad was crying out for help in the only way that he knew how. But I didn't understand that then . . . all I felt was anger towards him.

'My parents had been unhappily married for some time but one day the situation erupted. My dad's background didn't help: he grew up in an environment where men were considered both a waste of space and a waste of time. Apparently, his mother and sister were very domineering. Eventually, my grandfather ended up in a wheelchair and needed a lot of help, which put a further strain on family relationships and reinforced the idea that men were weak and had little to contribute. Hence they were shown little respect and were made to feel inadequate.

'When my father first met my mother, she couldn't speak much English because she came from another country. In those days she was very vulnerable and so, for the first time in his life, my father could be the man of the house – that was until she learned to speak English. Then, because she's from a different culture, she became very domineering and he slunk back into his old habits and began to do silly, irresponsible things again, like not paying his taxes.

'Things became really inflamed when one day my mother received a telephone call from a man who said he had warned my father that if he didn't leave his girlfriend alone he would phone his wife and tell her what her husband was doing behind her back. But we later found out that this girl was an alcoholic and my father was trying to "help" her by taking her out for meals and buying her drinks. He was trying to befriend her in his own funny sort of way, not realising he was making the other man extremely jealous at the same time.

'When I was young my father used to be my hero, but suddenly my eyes were opened and he became a human being who was so imperfect, who would suddenly shout and scream and be totally out of control. Now I understand why he behaved like that. He wanted the attention that had always been denied him as a child and as a young man. He wanted to be appreciated. He wanted to be loved.

'So, in a bid to escape the suffocating atmosphere at home, I left England and went abroad to work in a hotel. I hated England, and I hated the English. I blamed everything on them. I even said I wasn't English! I was determined that I wasn't going to have anything to do with any of it.

'But in the hotel where I was working, everything seemed to be going wrong there too due to bad management. However, I was determined to persevere and not give up again because I was very aware that I had already dropped out of university. I was going to prove to my family that I was actually going to do something worthwhile.

'I was feeling very unhappy, though, and one day decided

to go for a walk in the park to think things over. The pressure of staying on in this job just to prove a point was making me miserable. Just as I was strolling along, lost in my own thoughts, a man came up behind me and the next thing I knew I was being attacked in broad daylight. He wrestled me to the ground, but I reacted instinctively. Having had brothers, I knew how to fight and make a noise. Anger surged into me. How *dare* this man attack me. I screamed as loudly as I could and my screams attracted some attention, and the attacker ran off. It was all over in a few seconds and I wasn't hurt; but I was shocked.

'On returning home, I felt increasingly that everything seemed to be going wrong. I felt depressed and I didn't know what to do. So I decided to visit my aunt, who lived nearby. We had always got on well and she was somebody I felt would listen and help me decide what to do. By this time I had decided to return to England . . . the attack had finally convinced me that there was no point in me staying abroad.

'When I told my aunt that I was planning to go back to England, she said to me, "Would you like to go to a weekend called 'Believing in God'?" I was somewhat surprised! But it was a positive suggestion, so I went. It turned out to be amazing, and I met with God. As soon as I walked into the conference hall I could sense really powerfully the presence and the love of God. I didn't understand everything that was being said; some of it went over my head. But they were talking about how urgent it is to give your life to Jesus, and I just knew that whatever this thing was I had to do it; I wanted it. There was one girl there I got on particularly well with, and I asked her if she would pray with me.

'She spoke to me about one thing in particular –

forgiveness. She suggested I needed to ask forgiveness from God for the things that I had done wrong and then I needed to forgive those people who had hurt me, because if I didn't forgive them I would never be free in my spirit.

'I could accept what she said. It seemed to make sense. It was almost as if God had been preparing me because I had already started to forgive my dad even before I went away for the weekend. I had already begun calling him and speaking to him again. This girl prayed with me and asked God to show me the people I needed to forgive. He very clearly showed me three men in particular. One was my dad, the other was the man who attacked me in the park, and the other was a guy I had had a wrong relationship with. So I prayed and told God I was willing to forgive these people. Then we prayed again and asked God to show me the things in my life that I needed him to forgive.

'As children we were sent to a private school that had all sorts of philosophies. They described themselves as Christian, but really the focus was on the man who founded the school. It had begun with very good intentions for people who couldn't afford an education; today, though, you have to pay a lot of money to go there. I was at that school until the age of eighteen – and the school had greatly influenced my thinking. I now felt God wanted to free me from some of the ideas that had been planted in my mind from those days . . . ideas that had been based on the somewhat humanistic philosophy of the founder rather than biblical ideals; the two had become rather muddled and confused and I felt I needed to rethink some of my values. So she and I wrote that down.

'The second thing I asked forgiveness for concerned the wrong relationship I'd had with a guy. And finally, I felt God wanted me to ask his forgiveness for the way I had treated my father.

'Then I asked Jesus to come into my life. As we prayed, she explained it was like moving house. You have to take the old furniture out before you can move the new furniture in. And it just made sense to me. So we prayed it through and I just knew that it was right and that I wanted to believe in God. I knew that I had to forgive and be forgiven. I was determined to do it. It was as though God put his hand in me, took all the rubbish out, threw it away, and then Jesus came in and filled all the empty spaces that had been created. I was on an absolute high! That week was incredible. It was wonderful.

'Before that day I couldn't stop crying and then, after I'd prayed, I walked out and the world was just a beautiful place to be in and I was so glad I was there. Before that I was a desperately sad person. I kept thinking, what's the point of life? I was looking at the hotel and the way people were treating each other, and then at my parents and the way they treated each other, and always feeling responsible for them.

'I was twenty-one when I became a Christian and still living abroad. I felt I had to tell my family what had happened to me. First I had to face my mother's family, so I went to see my aunt and uncle who also lived abroad. All day long I didn't say a word about the weekend that had changed my life. My aunt was trying to be patient, but I waited until my uncle had gone to bed before I told her I had become a Christian and had given my life to Jesus, because I knew that he was very anti-God and Jesus.

'She couldn't believe it! She was very pleased. I was only the second person in the entire family to become a Christian; she was the first and I was the second.

'I had one more week abroad before I was due to return to

England. Now that I had met all these nice people, though, I didn't want to go back. But God said to me very clearly, "It's not the people that attract you, but it's Jesus in them and you will meet people like them in England."

'I didn't share my apprehension with my aunt, but before I left she said to me, "There's a good church near to where you are living, maybe they will have connections to churches in England." I took down the address of the church she gave me, but when I went looking for it, I couldn't find it. I didn't have much money in my purse, but I asked a taxi driver if he could take me there and how much it would cost. The amount he said was the exact amount I had in my purse! So I finally reached the church and went in.

'After the service I went to the back of the church to look at the notice board for information about churches in England. But there was nothing and I felt disappointed. It was raining so I decided to go back to where I was living and asked a lady for directions to the railway station. However, for some reason, she offered me a lift in her car. On the way she asked me what I was doing in the country. I told her I was planning to go back to England and that I was looking for a good church there.

' "I can't believe it," she said, "I was going to go to a Revival conference in England this weekend and I couldn't go; but now I have met you I know why! Here's the address – you have got to go to that church." And "that church" is the church I have been going to ever since!

'My mum lived close to this church. So when I came back to England I went to stay with her and the first thing I did was go to this church. But I was in for a horrible shock. They were praying loudly in tongues and I thought they were all mad and couldn't wait to leave. Towards the end of the service, somebody asked if there were any visitors and my hand just went up. Two students came to talk to me. One was from Ghana, and I had been travelling round Ghana so knew the country, and the other one was from Manchester and she was a very nice girl. I got on well with both of them and before I left they prayed with me. After that, everything changed and I couldn't wait to go back to the church the next week. The following year I became a student at the Bible College there!

'All this while, I was living with my mother. It was not an easy situation because she decided my church was a cult! I had come back from living abroad very enthusiastic and full of God and I was determined that I was going to grab everyone in my family by the scruff of their necks and drag them into the kingdom of God! Fortunately, I soon realised that that wasn't the way to do it. My mum thought I was getting involved with some very weird and dangerous people and started trying to persuade me to leave, but the more she tried to persuade me, the more I got involved.

'Before this, my mum and I had always been very close. But my new faith and her opinions were driving us apart. Then one day, as I was praying, Jesus gave me a vision of the umbilical cord that joined me to my mum being cut, and instead I was being joined to Jesus. I knew that he was going to do it. It was very, very hard though. Looking back, in many ways I had always been intimidated and manipulated by my mum so that I would always do what she wanted. She could make me feel intensely guilty at any time. But God freed me from that and I continued to live with her for the next eight months.

'By this time, one of my brothers was at university while the other one was living at home, and while I had been abroad, my brother at home had started taking drugs. By now my father had been legally forced to move out of the family house, but I decided to rebuild the relationship with my dad, which had the effect of being very threatening to my mum. However, I told him I forgave him for all the disappointment he had caused me and we had a really good conversation; I then asked him to come to church with me the following Sunday. And he came! It was absolutely amazing. Somebody with a similar background to his gave their testimony and my father gave his life to Jesus that day.

'So why did I need to forgive him? For letting me down. And I forgave him for not being there to protect and discipline me. That was one of the biggest things lacking in all of our lives. Our father was often not there at all, and when he was, it was just very difficult.

'I don't think he was expecting me to call him to say I'd forgiven him. He thought I was a bit off my head! He enjoyed it because I was obviously showing him love. I was explaining spiritual things to him, which he understood and made sense to him, and he began to understand why things had happened to him. I began building him up. God told me to respect my father.

'We then took a trip away together. God specifically told me to go away on holiday with my father and not to make one decision myself, but to let my dad make every single decision and to let him do whatever he wanted to do. It was very hard for both of us, because my dad just couldn't handle making his own decisions. He was so used to women taking control and telling him what was going to happen. But God helped me to be very patient.

'Forgiving my dad made a huge difference to my life. It made me feel so free. I was completely unburdened. And now I have no animosity towards the people who have hurt me –

none at all. With my mum it's been a long drawn-out process, because when I came back to England there were so many things I couldn't understand. I had received this wonderful gift of faith in God and she just wasn't taking any of it – she didn't want it, she didn't want to know; I think she was scared of it. Obviously my faith was taking me away from her and she didn't like that. She went away for a week and told me, "Your father is not to come in this house while I'm away, not one footstep in this house." I was torn because on the one hand he was taking me to church because I didn't have any transport, but on the other hand I had to say to him, "You're not allowed in this house." So I prayed very hard, "God, help me, because on the one hand I want to obey my mum . . . I want to do what she wants even if I don't believe it's right, but on the other hand I don't want to hurt my dad again." And God gave me a wonderful idea. I said to my dad, "This is what Mummy said, she doesn't want you in the house, but that's OK, we have to respect that because she is obviously scared or whatever. So, we are going to have a picnic in the car." And so we did, we had a brilliant time. We had a picnic in the car and it was absolutely wonderful.

'I have had to ask God to help me to forgive my mother again and again and again, but also I have had to apologise to her one hundred thousand times! It says in the Bible that we must forgive seventy times seven, and even the other day I had to apologise again even though I felt I was in the right; I had realised that the reaction inside me wasn't right because I got frustrated.

'I have also had to learn to forgive myself. When I gave my life to Jesus and repented of all my sins, I knew he had forgiven me. I had a very real sense of "I'm forgiven". I'm loved, I belong. He's my Father and I'm his child. But every now and then the memories overwhelmed me. I don't know if I blamed myself for my parents' marriage falling apart, but I always felt responsible for my parents. If they screamed or shouted at each other I was there; I couldn't do my homework because I had to be around making sure they didn't hit each other. When I was seventeen, things reached an all-time low between them and my mum shared my room and my bed for six months. Then my brother came into our room as well because he wanted to be with us; so for about four months the three of us were there together. I felt I was the one trying to keep the whole thing OK. I always felt very responsible for my family and that's something that I have had to learn to let go of. I think that's why today I have a heart for helping unhappy children.

'My priority now is to serve God and to give him absolutely everything. I know that I am only here now because of God. When I became a Christian he gave me a promise, "That me and my household will be saved and serve the Lord." I'm seeing it coming to fulfilment because one of my brothers is now a very strong Christian and is planning to go to Bible College. My other brother is getting closer without knowing it. I just know that God has also promised me that he will restore my mother's and father's relationship. I know that I can entrust them into his hands and leave all of that behind and go and serve him.

'I would love to get married one day and have my own children, because I think there is something so beautiful and very precious about family life. I believe I will.'

10

Reciprocal Forgiveness
– Joyce Lamb

As a child, Joyce Lamb was abused and intimidated by her alcoholic, violent father. A quiet, modest woman, Joyce Lamb's demeanour betrays the fact that she is a powerful woman of God. Working alongside her husband David, together they pastor the Ashford Christian Fellowship in Kent. David, too, has his own remarkable story to tell. But as this is a book about forgiveness, we are concentrating on Joyce's story – which is amazing not only because she forgave her father, but they were reconciled in a quite miraculous way. Joyce takes up the story:

'I was born in Malaysia in 1947. Malaysia is in south-east Asia and today is a cosmopolitan country. But when I was a child, Malaysia was ruled by the British, and it was the British who brought Christianity to my country. The British built mission schools, roads, church buildings, hospitals and they also introduced the English language to Malaysia.

'My grandparents (both my mother's and father's parents) emigrated from Sri Lanka (which was then known as Ceylon) to Malaysia. My father's side of the family were Hindus by background, while my mother's side of the family were Christian. My great-grandfather (on my mother's side) was a Hindu who later converted to Christianity and became an evangelist in Sri Lanka. He and his daughter (my grand-mother) used to visit the local villages preaching the gospel wherever they went. My grandmother and grandfather (on my mother's side) were Christians and they had a great influence on my life as I was growing up – they taught me about Jesus.

'And so it was that my father, who was from a Hindu background, married my mother, from a Christian back-ground. They were cousins (my father's mother and my mother's father were brother and sister). My mother's aunt (her father's sister) was the only one in the family who was a Hindu; this was because she married a Hindu man.

'My dad so desperately wanted to marry my mother that he told my grandparents he would convert and become a Christian. And so, true to his word, he was baptised in water (sprinkled) in the Methodist Church, and later married my mother in that same church. However, after their marriage he gradually stopped going to church, and also tried to stop my mum going too. But, bravely, my mum refused and continued to go without him. She faithfully took us children to Sunday school every week and at home she regularly read to us from the Bible and taught us to say the Lord's Prayer. If ever we were afraid, she used to make us repeat the Lord's Prayer after her.

'My grandparents (my mother's parents) used to live in a village near the town where we lived. Sometimes my father would take us as a family to their home on a Saturday; but he would leave us there, promising that he would return later to take us home. However, more often than not, he would come back very late at night to pick us up, and was always drunk. I can clearly remember being very afraid of travelling home with him when he was like this, and as children we used to tell our grandparents that we were afraid to go back home with him.

'But there wasn't a lot they could do and, invariably, on our journey home from my grandparents, my dad and mum would always quarrel, and my mum often threatened to open the door of the car and jump out. At times like this, my dad would drive very fast and we were flung from side to side in the back of the car as he turned the steering wheel erratically from left to right.

'We were so afraid that my mum would jump out of the car and kill herself that we cried all the way home. It was a horrible time. To give them credit, my grandparents had a prayer room in their house where they would take us and pray over us. They used to lay their hands on our heads and pray; this made me feel safe. I always welcomed those times when they did this. I think they must have been so worried about us travelling home with my father – it must have been very difficult for them.

'I specifically remember that when my dad was drunk he used to call us three children one by one and ask us who we loved most – Mummy or Daddy? We used to say "Mummy", and then he would threaten us, "What did you say?" Because we were so afraid of him, we used to say that we loved Daddy more than Mummy. There was always so much sadness when my dad was under the influence of alcohol. He could be violent, especially to my mum.

'In my early years I attended a Mission School in Malaysia, which was started by British Christian missionaries. Every Monday we had to attend a service in the chapel. I loved it and tried very hard not to miss those times. What I really loved most was the singing! My friends and I used to sit together and once the singing was over, we would secretly write notes to each other during the sermon! I never listened to the preacher because I thought I knew it all!

'Once a month our teacher took a count of how many Christians there were in each class so that the missionaries would know if anyone had accepted the Lord Jesus as their Saviour. During these counts I used to put my hand up to indicate that I was a Christian. All my friends knew that I would put up my hand when there was a count, and I used to feel proud to associate myself with the English.

'On one particular day, however, during the chapel service the speaker managed to capture my attention. This was because she asked if any of us were scared of dogs. In my country it was common for stray dogs to roam freely in the streets and, sometimes, if you were to ride a bicycle at speed past a dog, it would chase you!

'This once happened to me. I was riding a bicycle fast and a dog chased me, barking loudly. I was terrified and cried all the way home; from then on I was very afraid of dogs.

'So when the English missionary asked who was afraid of dogs, my ears pricked up. I started to listen. She continued, "You don't have to be scared because Jesus will help you. Say a quick prayer like 'Jesus save me' and he will come and save you." She said, "How many of you are Christians here?" I quickly put my hand up proudly. Then she went on to say, "You do know that you are not a Christian just because you go to church. You are not a Christian just because you pray."

I began to be more and more interested in her talk because I had never been told that before.

'By now I wanted to hear more. She said, "Jesus stands at the door of your heart and is knocking, and he is asking you to open your heart and let him in. He wants to live in your heart and change you from the inside." She asked another question, "How many of you find it difficult to love your brothers and sisters and are always fighting? And the more you don't want to fight, the more you end up fighting." Well, now she was *really* talking to me! This happened all the time! I wanted to change, but was unable to change myself. I used to vow daily and say to myself, "I am *not* going to fight with my brother and sister today!" I would try my best to get on with them, but I always failed and ended up fighting. I used to really struggle in this area.

'The speaker said, "If you are like this, and find yourself in this situation, Jesus can come into you and change your heart to help you stop fighting." She said that "Jesus will take your heart of stone and give you a new heart, the heart of Jesus to help you stop fighting with your brothers and sisters." She added, "Ask Jesus to forgive you all of your sins and invite him to come and live in your heart and change you." She went on to tell us that Jesus came to die for our sins and when we accept this and believe it, then we become Christians.

'It was then that I realised that I was not a Christian. I was so shocked at this revelation that I started to cry. The speaker then said, "How many of you want to become a Christian today?" I put my hand up. My friends who were seated next to me started to pull my hand down, saying, "She did not say how many Christians are *here*, but how many of you want *to become* Christians!" My friends told me to put my hand down

– they could not understand what had happened to me, or why I had put my hand up! I went forward in tears and gave my life to Jesus, because I was so grateful to him for what he did on the cross for me. So it was at that moment, aged twelve, that the Lord Jesus revealed himself to me as my Saviour.

'But my family and home background was not a very good one as you will by now have gathered. My father was an alcoholic and we seldom saw him sober. As children, we were often woken up in the early hours of the morning with the sound of shouting and crying. My dad often hit my mum. As we lay in bed, we could hear everything that was going on and we used to lie very still without making a sound so as not to draw attention to ourselves just in case he came over and hit us too. Words cannot describe the fear we lived with day after day, night after night, as we were growing up. There were times when we went to bed hungry because my dad had squandered his pay on alcohol, leaving my mother with no money to buy food.

'In Malaysia we had to pay school fees every month, and I remember many times asking my dad for this money. But he would often tell me off just for asking. I was so ashamed of him because he was different from my friends' fathers.

'From a very young age, I would write letters to Jesus. If there was a quarrel going on between my parents, or if I had been misunderstood, or told off for no reason, I would go to my room, shut my bedroom door, and write a letter to Jesus. I told Jesus all about how I felt, how I had been misunderstood, and how it hurt me seeing my mum and dad quarrelling all the time. After writing the letter, I would put it under the mattress and then often I would lie on the bed and fall into a deep sleep. When I woke up I felt so good and was able to face living again. I know now of course what must have happened to me during those times. Writing to Jesus was just like praying. Falling into a deep sleep was when Jesus ministered to me! This was a pattern I developed during those difficult times, and because of this pattern, even now, if I am upset or wronged by someone, I go straight to Jesus and tell him everything. So from when I was very young, Jesus became my best friend and confidant.

'I grew up actually hating my dad. I hated him because he brought sadness and misery to us children and to my mum. I was so ashamed of him. Consequently, my attitude towards him was horrible. If he wanted a cup of coffee, I would bring the cup of coffee reluctantly, throw it down on the table, and leave the room banging the door shut after me. Little did I know that I had allowed bitterness to take root in my life.

'One thing I always did after becoming a Christian was to pray for my dad, that God would change him and save him. I prayed every day without fail for years. But there was no change. I prayed that Jesus would sort him out and stop him drinking.

'When I was twenty-two years old, I had the opportunity of leaving Malaysia and coming to England, to train to be a nurse. I was so glad at that time to leave home, to get away from all the unhappiness. Another reason I was happy to come to England was because of my association with the English missionaries I had met as a child, and who had had such a positive influence on my life. So I came to know Jesus because of the faithfulness of these dear people. But because every English person I had met in Malaysia was a Christian, I therefore expected, naively, that everyone living in England would be a Christian too! I was so excited at the prospect of coming to England to get to know more Christians, and Jesus, in a deeper way. I dreamt about being a nurse and then using my training to become a missionary. That was my plan.

'I travelled to England with a friend who also wanted to be a nurse, and on our first day in our new surroundings we were taken to the hospital canteen to have our supper. We met a young Englishman with long red hair. He smiled at us and asked if he could share our table. We of course said he could. It turned out that he too was a nurse. He began the conversation by asking us,"Can't you train to become a nurse in your own country? Why have you come from so far away, from the other side of the world, to England, to train to be nurses?"

'I explained to this young red-haired man that we did have training schemes for nurses in Malaysia, but the reason I was here in England was because Jesus directed me to do my training here.

'The young man looked shocked and asked what my plans were after the training. I told him that I was going to become a missionary nurse and go wherever Jesus wanted me to go!

'He said, "You look too young to be a missionary. You are not one of those people who speak about Jesus, are you?"

'By now I was very shocked to hear an English person behave as though he didn't believe in Jesus! I was terribly disappointed, but I decided there and then that England would be my mission field! And from that day on, I began to talk to him about Jesus.

'While in England, I had continued to pray for my dad. One birthday, a friend called Gurnam Singh (Malaysian by birth) gave me a gift; it was a book by Catherine Marshall. I always enjoyed reading, and on my day off I began to read this book. As I read, the writer explained how we can negatively affect a person through unforgiveness and thus prevent Jesus from working in their lives. Catherine Marshall wrote that when we have unforgiveness in our hearts we are, in effect, binding that person – and that in turn can stop them from believing in Jesus.

'For the first time in my life I realised that my dad was bound by me, through my unforgiveness, and therefore he was unable to receive Jesus into his heart. After all these years, I realised I was the blockage!

'Around the same time, my mother phoned me from Malaysia. She told me that my dad was seriously ill and that the doctors had given up hope; he was dying. That news really shook me because if he were to die, I believed he would go to hell because of me!

'I wept because I recognised there was a deep, deep root of bitterness in me. In my teenage years I had developed pains in my knee joints, and I now believe it was because of the bitterness I felt towards my father.

'So I started to speak to Jesus about the situation and told him that it was my dad who had wronged me. I explained that my father was the one who needed to ask me for forgiveness! But the Lord told me that my attitude towards my dad was not right, and he showed me that I was not behaving as a daughter should. Jesus showed me how unkind I was being.

'I struggled with this. For years I thought I was the one who had been wronged; that it was all my father's fault. Eventually I decided to forgive my dad, but I found it hard. The Lord told me that the first step was for me to be willing to forgive and then he would help me.

'At first, I struggled a lot emotionally. Eventually, I did forgive my dad, but I did not feel any love towards him. I felt glad I had obeyed Jesus and forgiven my father; but that was all. However, God helped me; he backed up my decision to forgive with his ability to do it, and to my surprise the Lord told me to write to my dad and ask him to forgive me for my attitude towards him as a daughter.

'By now I had no contact with my father and we had certainly never written to each other! In fact, I had not spoken to him since leaving Malaysia to come to England. I couldn't remember my dad ever speaking any kind words to me and I had never heard him say "I love you". Maybe he did when I was very young, but I could not recall it. I struggled with all of this, but eventually I put pen to paper.

'At the same time, a man of God from India – an evangelist – was visiting Malaysia. One day, he was praying and God told him to go to a particular hospital in the town where my parents lived. Apparently God guided the man by telling him to turn right and left and took him straight to my father's bed! This man of God explained to my dad that while he had been praying, God had spoken to him and that he had been directed by the Holy Spirit to visit. He went on to explain that God wanted my dad to hear the truth. This holy man explained to my father how Jesus loved him. He also told him that because of God's love for him, he sent Jesus to die in place of us so that our sins can be forgiven and we can have a new start. He also explained to my dad that the Bible says "with his stripes we are healed" (Isa. 53:7, RSV). He added that if my dad would accept what Jesus had done on the cross for him, then his sins would be forgiven and he would be healed.

'My dad decided to accept what the man said and invited Jesus into his heart to change him. This man of God prayed for him and my dad was healed! He was discharged from the hospital to home, and wrote his first letter to me. I cried tears of joy as I read it. He asked me to forgive him! He explained in the letter about the visiting evangelist and all that he had told him and what had happened to him. I was so excited that my dad had finally made contact with me. I kept reading the letter over and over again, and suddenly my feelings towards him changed. Finally, after all those years of hatred, I felt I loved my father for the first time. I treasure that letter. It is so precious.

'The most exciting thing about this story was that our letters crossed in the post! The moment I forgave my dad, he was released to accept Jesus into his heart. Isn't the Lord Jesus wonderful? Jesus brought us together. It would not have happened without Jesus. I learnt a very important lesson about the power of forgiveness through this experience.

'It was as though I had been clutching dirty rags, and these dirty rags were my dad's sins. Imagine holding someone else's sins in your own heart. Holding on to his wrongs. That is why I became bitter.

'Through this experience I learnt that when we ask Jesus for forgiveness, he forgives us. And he not only forgives us, but he also forgets the sin. So Jesus forgives and forgets! And Jesus wanted me to be like him; I had to understand for myself that his character is to forgive and forget. So Jesus forgave and forgot my father's sins when he asked him to do so that day in the hospital, and now with God's help I was able to do the same. The bitterness has now gone, rooted out by the power of forgiveness. My heart has healed and Jesus has shown his deep love for me and my dad, and now I have such peace. The depth of his healing was indescribable, sufficient to say I was made whole; for the first time in my life I felt absolutely complete. All the sorrow has gone. I live without any regrets.

'To return to the red-haired Englishman whom I met on the first day I arrived in England. When I realised that he was not a Christian, I started to pray for him and to tell him about Jesus. Every time I met him I spoke to him about Jesus. He must have got very fed up with me, because one day he told me to stop speaking to him about Jesus. So I did – and decided to pray for him instead!

'Soon after, he became ill and was taken to the sick bay. So I visited him every day. One particular occasion I had received a magazine written by Selwyn Hughes, and I took this magazine with me so that I would have something to read while I sat with him. When I entered the room he asked me about the magazine. I told him that it would not be of interest to him because it was about Jesus! When the time came for me to leave, I was prompted by the Holy Spirit to leave the magazine on the table. So I did. My English acquaintance started to be uncomfortable and told me to take the magazine away with me. But I told him just to leave it, and that I would come and pick it up after work. Then I left and went on my way.

'After work I forgot about the magazine and went home. Early the next morning, the Englishman knocked on my door. I was very surprised to see him. He had discharged himself from the hospital and looked terribly shocked. I asked him what he was doing at my door, and he said, "You never told me that Jesus is coming again; I read about it in the magazine you left in the sick bay." I was surprised that he had even looked at the magazine and reminded him that I had told him many times that Jesus was coming again; it was just that he had seen it for the first time! It was a Sunday; he was agitated and told me that he was going to find a church. But I was very concerned that he went to the right church; after all this, I wanted to make sure he got the message!

'Somehow I managed to find the administrating nursing officer, who was a Christian, to accompany him. Together they went to the local Elim Church – and guess what the pastor preached about? He preached on the second coming! Needless to say, that was the Englishman's special day! He became a Christian, and after that we became really good friends; and eventually David – this young Englishman – asked me to marry him!

'David wanted to ask my father for my hand in marriage. People from Sri Lanka at that time were often prejudiced about marrying into a race other than their own. In the past, my father would have flatly refused; but now he was so different, he was a changed man. So when David asked him, his reply was amazing, "If he loves Jesus, he can marry you. I will give my consent." This was a staggering miracle!

'David and I had our wedding ceremony in West Malaysia, with over 500 guests in attendance. Our full-time ministry started after that, and twenty-seven years later we are still serving Jesus together as pastors in Ashford, Kent.

'My father lived for many years after that. The alcohol and violence became things of the past and he shared his new-found belief with our Hindu relatives. He would speak to them for hours at a time about the love of Jesus Christ.

'Some time later, he started to have difficulty with his breathing and was taken to hospital. They gave him oxygen to ease his condition and by the next day he was feeling better. He was told that the following day he would be discharged and able to return home. My mum was with him in the hospital that day and, as he was talking to her, he leaned back in the bed. But suddenly he sat up and said to her, "Shhh . . . Where is that beautiful music coming from?" My mother looked at the hospital radio earphones to see if they were switched on. But no sound was coming out of them; the radio was switched off. He told my mother he could hear a lovely choir – beautiful music. This carried on for ten minutes and my mum thought he was losing his mind.

'Then he told her that God had spoken to him and said, "Today I am taking you home and the music you are hearing is music from heaven." He then asked my mum to forgive him for the horrible life he had given her. He said to her, "If I had my life again, I would treat you like a queen." He also told her to make sure that we, his children, knew that he had asked God to forgive him. He spoke each one of our names and said how pleased he was that we all loved Jesus.

'In the evening, my father's sisters came to visit him. They encouraged my mum to go home and have a rest while they stayed with my dad. He kept telling his sisters, with a big smile on his face, "They have opened the windows and there are lights everywhere. They are ready for my entry now!" Then he died.

'He is with Jesus and one day I will see him again. I am looking forward in anticipation to that great day.'

Conclusion

I wonder if I might have one last word with you before you put this book down? I wish I could be right there with you and see if there might be a need for you to make a definite commitment regarding total forgiveness. I want you to think about who you need to forgive. You probably already have done this. When I preach my sermon on total forgiveness, which I have done in the United Kingdom, Australia, Iraq, Alaska and all over the United States, I end the sermon by asking for people to make a public commitment. I am going to ask you if you will do this.

Here is what I want you to do. If you have been convicted by the Holy Spirit that you have a real need to forgive – of which you may not have been aware when you began the book, I believe you should act on this – now. Here is why. If you don't, the devil will come alongside and persuade you either to postpone this commitment or sweep the whole matter under the carpet – and you may never feel the same as you do at the moment. I want to you promise God, with the angels observing, that you will forgive that person – that you will truly set them free and pray for them.

But before you make such a commitment, please note carefully what you must be willing to do. First, you promise that you will not tell what 'they' did. You may say, 'It's too late, I've already done that.' I answer: just don't do it any more! Second, you promise you will not cause them to be afraid of you – you won't let them be intimidated. Third, you won't let them feel guilty. Fourth, you will let them save face. Fifth, you will protect them from their fear of a secret being told. Sixth, you accept that total forgiveness is a life sentence – you must keep on dong it. Finally, you will pray for them – to be blessed.

If you are ready, I will ask you to pray this prayer (it would be good if you could pray it aloud). Don't pray this prayer unless you mean it because God will take you seriously.

Lord Jesus Christ, I need you. I want you. I am sorry for my sins. Wash my sins away by your blood. I am sorry for my bitterness. I am sorry for holding a grudge.

I now forgive [insert the name of the person or people]. I will not tell what they did. I will not let them be afraid of me. I will not let them feel guilty. I will let them save face. I will protect them from their worst fear. I accept that this matter of forgiving is something I will keep on doing – it is a life sentence. I now pray for them. I ask you to bless them. I set them free.

Thank you for your patience with me. I welcome your ungrieved Spirit into my heart. As best as I know how, I give you my life. Amen.

God bless you. May the richest blessing of the Blessed Trinity – Father, Son and Holy Spirit – be upon you from this day and as long as you live. Amen.